A PRIVATE JOURNAL OF
JOHN GLENDY SPROSTON, U.S.N.

A MONUMENTA NIPPONICA
MONOGRAPH

A PRIVATE JOURNAL OF
JOHN GLENDY SPROSTON U.S.N.

EDITED BY SHIO SAKANISHI

WITH A NEW FOREWORD BY

GEORGE ALEXANDER LENSEN

SOPHIA UNIVERSITY · TOKYO

IN COOPERATION WITH

CHARLES E. TUTTLE COMPANY

RUTLAND, VERMONT & TOKYO, JAPAN

REPRESENTATIVES
Continental Europe: BOXERBOOKS, INC., *Zurich*
British Isles: PRENTICE-HALL INTERNATIONAL, INC., *London*
Australasia: PAUL FLESCH & Co., PTY. LTD., *Melbourne*
Canada: M. G. HURTIG, LTD., *Edmonton*

Published by Sophia University
7, Kioi-chō, Chiyoda-ku, Tokyo
in cooperation with
Charles E. Tuttle Company, Inc.
of Rutland, Vermont & Tokyo, Japan
with editoral offices
at Suido 1-chōme, 2-6, Bunkyo-ku, Tokyo

Library of Congress Catalog Card No. 68-29831
First published, 1940
Second Edition, revised and reset, 1968

PRINTED IN JAPAN

PETER BROGREN, THE VOYAGERS' PRESS, TOKYO

FOREWORD

by George Alexander Lensen

IN 1940 *Sophia University in Tokyo brought out the first volume of a projected series of eyewitness accounts of early American-Japanese relations. The manuscripts scheduled for publication were important not only because they filled gaps in historical knowledge, but because they contained, in the words of Dr. J. B. Kraus, S. J., then editor of* Monumenta Nipponica, *'many a useful lesson for our own time how to maintain and improve peaceful relations between the two great Pacific nations even in an atmosphere sometimes clouded and infected by misunderstanding and distrust.' But the misunderstanding and distrust had already exceeded the bounds of reason and the series fell victim to the Japanese-American holocaust which it had sought to forestall.*

The bloodletting drained the two powers not only of strength but of hatred and before long the two countries were, generally speaking, on better and closer terms than they had ever been before. The majestic figure of General Douglas MacArthur symbolized the Occupation much as that of Commodore Matthew Calbraith Perry had the Opening of Japan. To what extent MacArthur may have consciously patterned his conduct after Perry I do not know, but there can be no doubt that he was familiar with Perry's theatrical bearing and its success in Japan.

With the centennial of the opening of Japan interest was revived in the Perry expedition and a number of eyewitness accounts were published individually, including works originally considered for inclusion in the Early American-Japanese Relations Series. But while they found readers in the United States, particularly when published and publicized there, the Private Journal of John Glendy Sproston, *which had been printed in Tokyo on the eve of the Pacific War on poor paper, remained forgotten. The centennial of the Meiji Restoration has once more focussed attention on nineteenth century Japan and the time seems ripe to republish the observations of the young American naval officer who participated in the opening of Japan.*

GEORGE ALEXANDER LENSEN

TOKYO, MARCH, 1968

CONTENTS

APPENDIX

LIST OF ILLUSTRATIONS

Editor's Introductory Note

THOSE who were acquainted with the documentary sources of Commodore Perry's *Narrative of the Expedition of an American Squadron to the China Seas and Japan* were slightly puzzled when "an original manuscript by an officer of Perry squadron," which presumably was not known to the Commodore, appeared on the market in 1926. It will be recalled that at the beginning of the expedition, Commodore Perry gave strict orders to those under his command not to communicate with any one in regard to the movements of the Squadron or its discipline and regulations. These topics were to be avoided in private letters, and to make certain that the command was enforced, the letters were censored. Journals and notes kept by members of the expedition were to be looked upon as belonging to the government. Therefore, at the end of the expedition in August, 1854, in Hongkong, they were collected and sent to the Navy Department on the U.S.S. *Mississippi*. Mr. Francis L. Hawks, who edited the *Narrative*, makes acknowledgement to them in the 'Prefatory Note,' but adds that the Commodore's journals and correspondence form much the larger part. After the task was completed, all the private papers were returned to their respective owners.

A Private Journal of John Glendy Sproston, a manuscript folio of 105 pages in the original half calf, was noted for the first time in the *Catalogue* of the Anderson Galleries,[1] New York, in 1926, and was purchased by the Library of Congress. The consigner of the manuscript was not disclosed, and since then notwithstanding inquiries at the Galleries and elsewhere, it has not yet been possible to trace its history.

The U.S.S. *Macedonian* which had sailed from New York on April 11, 1853, joined the Squadron after much delay on February 14, 1854, at the American Anchorage in Edo Bay, and Sproston lost no time in recording the activities of the expedition. After a brief preliminary mention of the purpose of the present visit, he began his journal with

[1] See: Appendix, 7.

Captain Henry A. Adams' interview with the Japanese commissioners on the following morning in Kanagawa, and closed it eight months later in Hongkong only because he had an opportunity of forwarding it to his family in Baltimore through his friend, Kidder Randolph Breese. News from home took six to ten months to reach members of the expedition. Sproston wrote, 'Many changes of more or less importance have, no doubt, taken place, and the mind becomes anxious to know what they may be.' Fearing he might not have another chance of sending it in a near future, he entrusted the rough draft of his manuscript with a note: 'Sent in an unfinished state; will correct on reaching home, if I live.' Sproston lived through the strenuous duty of the East India Squadron, which lasted two more years after the conclusion of the Japan expedition, and returned home safely in 1856, but never had time to go back to his journal. Consequently, many foreign words and proper names, of which he was not certain, were left blank, except for one or two initial letters. Luckily, through existing sources in English and Japanese, it was possible to supply them.

It is difficult to believe that Sproston developed a sudden urge to keep such a detailed journal in Japan. He must have been in the habit of noting his impressions and experiences, and we regret that none of his letters and other journals have come down to us. That he had a taste for literature and, to some extent, literary talent, both he himself and his friend Breese, as well as the readers of the present journal, would grant. In this he hails the warmer weather when he can lounge on deck and indulge in reading. He would compose short epigramatic poems as he watched the rainbow; indulge in philosophical speculation as to the advantages of civilized or primitive life. He complains of the difficulty of writing on ship board, especially on the temperamental Japan Sea. Navigating unknown waters with the personnel cut to the minimum, calls of duty for the officers are frequent and strenuous. Yet he would not trade that life with anything else. 'Our long absence,' he writes, 'from fresh beef and civilization, though the cause of present discomfort, will ultimately prove a source of satisfaction to all concerned.'

Sproston's pen and pencil sketches excellently illustrate his text, and it is a matter for regret that there are only a few. He intended to draw many more and left space for them in the manuscript, but was not able to go back to them. In fact, several of his drawings are only in outline and half-finished.

Sproston is accurate in presenting facts which check well with those mentioned in Perry's *Narrative*, but his journal is limited in scope and contains nothing which is not recorded in the latter. Its distinguishing quality, however, consists of his personal observations and comments, although naturally being under the restrictions imposed by the Commodore it had to be very discreet, and hence uninteresting. He characterizes the unpopular Commodore Perry with a sentence, 'No one appreciates a joke less than he does.' Samuel Wells Williams, interpreter, is dismissed as 'properly a missionary in China and a remarkably disagreeable man.' Sproston's description of the last episode in Edo Bay, when the Commodore Perry tried to force his way to Edo, is much more dramatic than that in the *Narrative*. A young Japanese interpreter on the U.S.S. *Mississippi* actually became ill when he saw the course of the Squadron and was ready to commit *harakiri*. Throwing his cloak and long sword to an American officer, he said, 'Take them, for I have no more need of them. My short sword will be all that I shall require.' Commenting on an apparent lack of reciprocal faith and understanding on the part of the Japanese, Sproston concludes: 'For the great misfortune attending the propagation of civilization and Christianity among heathens is that the class of foreigners with whom they first come in contact are actuated only by motives of gain, irrespective of the method by which it is obtained.' Yet Sproston is very hopeful, for he writes that, 'In all probability before many years, hundred of ships will pass through these island groups in the California and China trade.'

A short description of a visit to the coal field in the vicinity of Keelung, Formosa, is written by Kidder Randolph Breese and perhaps is the dullest part of the journal, since it is given up almost entirely to one small incident before he started on the excursion and to the expression of his personal feelings.

Edward M. Barrows, who quotes from the present journal, assumes that Sproston kept his diary concealed. I do not know on what authority he based his assumption. At the end of his writing, Breese jokingly adds the following: 'My observation will be noted down and, I hope, handed down to posterity as they certainly ought to, and when Commodore Perry sees this book which I shall certainly recommend him to do, he will acknowledge the truth of it.' The fact that the manuscript was sent on the *Mississippi*, the flag ship of the U.S. Expedition to Japan, leads one to believe that the journal was known at least to Captain Joel Abbot, and that Sproston was permitted to send it back to his family through his good friend, Kidder Randolph Breese.

Biographical Note

JOHN Glendy Sproston was born in Baltimore, Maryland, on August 14, 1828. His father, George Saxon Sproston, served as a surgeon in the U. S. Navy from November 8, 1813, to January 27, 1842, the date of his death. His mother was Jane Glendy, third daughter of the Reverend John Glendy, a native of Londonderry, Ireland, who came to the United States in 1798 at the age of forty-three. Rev. Glendy became the first pastor of the Second Presbyterian Church in Baltimore in 1804 and retired in 1826. He was a close friend of President Thomas Jefferson. In 1805, Rev. Glendy was chaplain of the House of Representatives, and in 1815, and 1816, chaplain of the U. S. Senate. He died in Philadelphia on October 4, 1832.

George Saxon Sproston and Jane Glendy were married in Philadelphia on November 15, 1827, and settled in Baltimore. John Glendy was their first child, and he seems to have had two younger brothers: George Saxon Sproston, a paymaster on the U.S.S. *Marmora* in 1863 and chief clerk in the Bureau of Equipment and Recruiting, Navy Department, from 1892 to 1895, and William Glendy Sproston of whom little is known. His mother presumably lived at 95 South Charles Street, Baltimore, until her death on September 3, 1866. Beside his father and brother, John Glendy Sproston had an uncle in the U.S. Navy, William M. Glendy, who enlisted on January 1, 1818, and retired on July 16, 1862.

John Glendy Sproston was appointed a midshipman in the U.S. Navy from the state of Ohio on July 15, 1846, and was ordered to the U.S.S. *Independence* which was preparing for duty on the Pacific coast. This gave him active service in the Mexican War. He returned to the United States in April, 1847, because of ill health. His next service was on the U.S.S. *Brandywine* off the coast of Brazil from September, 1847, to December, 1850. On July 24, 1848, he was warranted a passed midshipman.

From February to August, 1851, Sproston served on the U.S.S. *St. Lawrence,* and from her went to the Naval Academy for a short period. From 1852 to 1856 he was an officer of the U.S.S. *Macedonian,* one of the vessels composing the fleet which carried out the first American expedition to Japan. The frigate *Macedonian* was commanded by the able Captain Joel Abbot (1793–1855) whom Commodore M. C. Perry ordered to visit the Japanese, Bonin, and Philippine island groups, as well as Formosa. Thus during the spring and summer of 1854 Sproston was fortunate enough to visit many of the unexplored places in the Far East. In August, 1854, when the main force of the Squadron was about to return home, Sproston chose to remain with the East India Squadron, commanded by Captain Abbot. He was made Acting Master of the Chartered Steamer *Queen* and Flag Officer of the Squadron. He returned home in August, 1856, and was assigned to duty on the Receiving Ship at Baltimore. Previous to his return on September 16, 1855, Sproston was promoted to lieutenant.

From 1857 to January, 1860, Lieutenant Sproston was again in the East Indies with the U.S.S. *Mississippi,* and upon his return home he was ordered to the Naval Rendezvous at Baltimore.

On April 28, 1861, Lieutenant Sproston was ordered to take command of the U.S.S. *Powhatan* for duty along the Virginia coast and inland waters. Later in the year, probably in June, he was transferred to the U.S.S. *Colorado* and about the first of October went to the U.S.S. *Seneca,* one of the vessels of the South Atlantic Blockading Squadron, as executive officer. He was killed June 8, 1862, at St. John's River in Florida while in command of an expedition sent ashore to capture a rebel captain named George Huston.

The steamer *Arago* brought the remains of Lieutenant Sproston from Hilton Head to New York on June 16, and he was interred in Greenmount Cemetery in Baltimore. 'An able, brave and devoted officer from the state of Maryland,' wrote Rear-Admiral S. F. Du Pont in an official memorandum.

The chief sources of information concerning John Glendy Sproston are contained in the Office of Naval Records and Library in the Navy Department at Washington. Details of his early life are completely lacking. All the members of the Glendy and Sproston families mentioned above are buried in Greenmount Cemetery which was opened in the latter part of 1839. At the office of the cemetery I have learned that many of them died outside of Maryland and were brought back for interrment later. The inscriptions on the stones are in many cases so worn that it is difficult to decipher them. The two families appear to have had a definite association with Philadelphia, but assiduous search among the records and newspaper files have failed to disclose any facts.

A PRIVATE JOURNAL OF

JOHN GLENDY SPROSTON, U.S.N

Sent in an unfinished state, not expecting to have an opportunity of forwarding it so soon. Will correct on reaching home, if I live.

SPROSTON

EIGHT MONTHS AFTER ITS COMMENCEMENT

'MACEDONIAN', HONGKONG, SEPT., 1854

At the
American Anchorage
Yedo Bay

THE intent of this expedition, viz. of establishing a commercial treaty with these singular people who have heretofore so secluded themselves from intercourse with foreign nations as to be truly an isolated empire, has now commenced on the part of our Commodore with spirit and determination, and I sincerely hope with ultimate success.

Captain Adams[1] and suite who attended the interview at Uraga,[2] were informed that the President's letter[3] had been favourably rec[d]. This town (Uraga) is about ten miles below Perry Island,[4] which is about six miles from our present anchorage, called the American Anchorage on account of our squadron (which then consisted of only two steamers and two sloops) having anchored here on their first visit. The Commodore held his interview outside of the town. Since then they have built and fitted up a house about fifty feet square, in which to hold all future intercourse; but the Commodore, from reasons of his own, and no doubt just ones, refused to attend there in person, and sent his fleet captain to represent him offering to send a steamer for the Japanese Prince,[5] who declined.

Captain Adams was politely rec[d]., but informed that Uraga must be the place to negotiate. With this answer he returned aboard the *Vandalia*. But whilst she was getting under way, the Japanese rec[d]. notice of the squadron's proceeding up the Bay, which caused them to immediately rescind the former reply to one more favourable.

In the meantime we had a party surveying the harbours and bays near. Determined the position of Webster Island;[6] found it to be in Lat. [35° 18′ 30″ N.] Long. [130° 40′ 34″ N.]. Between this island

---

[1] Commander Henry A. Adams (*d.* 1869), fleet captain.

[2] On board the *Powhatan*, Feb. 15. 1854.

[3] President Millard Fillmore's letter of credence delivered to the officials of the Shogunate on July 14, 1853.

[4] Saru-shima.

[5] Ki Hayashi (1799–1856), rector of the University of Yedo, was appointed by the Shogunate as the head commissioner of the negotiation.

[6] Natsu-shima.

A

and the main shore, surveyed a snug harbour open only to the north-ward and easterly, carrying five fathoms well up, in which we found beds of fine oysters, wild ducks, and near the villages, on the shores, wells and small springs of pure water. We landed and had our picnic dinner, climbed over the hills and visited the small towns on the op-posite side, found hazel-nuts and chestnuts in the woods, the doctor[7] and myself losing our way among them (I tumbling down and running a piece of bamboo through my hand). Visited their temples, which were small and contained two or three rudely carved idols, but were surrounded with fine large fir and cedar trees which gave a picturesque appearance to their otherwise unadorned places of worship.

Experiencing frequent gales, principally from N. E. and S. W., the movements of the squadron were im[paired] thereby; but as soon as it cleared off, all the ships except our own proceeded up the Bay about twelve miles, and anchored in a large secure harbour off the town of Kanagawa or Kang on the sea side.[8] We remained below to pilot up the *Saratoga*, expected daily from Shanghai. The *Vandalia* came up in the evening of the same day and joined the squadron.

Our ship remained at anchor off Webster Island several days after the departure of the squadron, during which time we were busily engaged touching up ship outside with paint, shifting sails, and per-forming the various duties belonging to a man-of-war, and which add so much to her general appearance as well as to the comfort of her officers. Sent out 'dingey' for a few beakers of spring water on Webster Island every day. Most of the water that we got on board at Loo Choo was slightly brackish, which made this the more acceptable. Every night, and often close to the shore, fires were to be seen,[9] which, judging from accounts and the combustible material used in building, must have been caused by the burning of Japanese dwellings.

On a clear moonlight night the snow-clad 'Volcano of Foesi' (Huzi)[10] would appear rising majestically above all surrounding land, but far in the distance. I would like much to have an opportunity of ascending to its summit some day.

The above* represents the harbour which we surveyed inside of Webster Island, which is represented in the foreground. We carried five fathoms well up; and for the most part in mid-channel, nine fa-

---

[7] Doctor Robert Woodworth, the senior medical officer.

[8] Kanagawa.

[9] By the order of the Shogunate, along the coast of the Miura Peninsula where the Amer-ican squadron anchored, watch-fires were burnt nightly and a system of signals organized.

[10] Mount Fuji.

* A blank space with no drawing.

thoms. The entrance is on the left hand. On the offshore and half-way
up the hill is the position of the temple represented at the top of the
page. A second one that we visited had an ascent of about fifty steps,
but time did not permit of my sketching it.

Orders came at last for us to get under way and join the squadron,
which we did with a light head-wind. In the course of the day we picked
up fifteen large logs of hard pine, about a foot and a half square and
twelve feet in length which kept the carpenters and a gang of hands
busily engaged sawing it into pieces of the required length and splitting it up for fire-wood. It amounted in all to more than eight cords.
At sundown, the wind dying away, and the strong flood which had
been making, slackening, we anchored.

On the following day beat in and anchored near the Commodore.
For several succeeding days experienced foggy, rainy weather with
constant northerly and northeast winds. Saw the buildings going up on
the shore for the reception of the Commodore, which looked like something definite. The surveying party surveyed the harbour, which
proved to be excellent, and planted buoys at regular intervals for each
ship of the squadron.

In obedience to general signal each vessel kedged up to and moved
in her appointed berth, the whole forming a crescent. About this time
the *Saratoga* joined us, having had a boisterous passage from Loo
Choo of three or four weeks, two of which were passed among the
Japan Islands during which they experienced heavy head-gales and
cold stormy weather. We now presented a very imposing aspect,[11]
and the music of the bands morning and evening, together with the
clang of bells and the numerous calls of the sentries and lookouts at
night, by no means decreased the effect upon the minds of the Japanese,
who evidently consider us a great nation.

MARCH 8TH

THIS day, if it be not hereafter remembered by our own, will at least
be long kept in mind by the people of this country. The morning
opened clear and pleasant with a light northeasterly wind, which died
away entirely in the latter part of the forenoon. In the morning watch,
I noticed the Japanese erecting a fence from the landing to the House of

---

[11] Now the entire squadron consisting of three steamers, the *Susquehanna*, *Powhatan*, *Mississippi*, and five vessels, the *Vandalia*, *Macedonian*, *Lexington*, *Saratoga*, and *South-ampton*, was in the Bay.

Reception. This, I knew, was contrary to the express desire of the Commodore who stated to them that he would not land if they did so; and a few minutes after, a gig left the flag-ship and pulled to the landing, which resulted in the fence being taken down.[12]

At 11 a.m. thirty boats belonging to the several ships of the squadron formed in line near the flag-ship and in prescribed order pulled for the landing in line about Captain Buchanan[13] leading in his gig (he having charge of the military proceedings of the day). Reaching the landing, disembarked the marine and body of armed seamen picked out for the occasion.

About this time the *Macedonian*, which had been sprung broadside to, fired a salute of seventeen guns. The marine gaurd were drawn up on the left and the seamen on the right, leaving a space of about a hundred feet in between the two, forming two columns stretching from the water's edge to the entrance of the main building, with bands of music at each end—bass and small drums, fifes, and so forth, arranged near the troops. The boats hauled off, anchored in what was intended to be a line thirty yards from the beach. In the middle of the line were twelve launches, each mounting a howitzer, intended for saluting.

The sight now was certainly a pleasing one. From the House of Reception, about one hundred yards, sloping very gradually to the water's edge, were drawn up the troops as I before mentioned: the marines, 160 in number in full dress, their arms glittering in the sun; opposite to them the sailors, 224 in number, in blue jackets and trousers, and blue caps with bands of red, white, and blue, with stars worked in the blue stripe. Their arms consisted of musket, pistol, and cutlass.

The white barge with the blue broad pennant now approached. As it passed the boats, the officers and men rose and took off their caps, a mark of respect. As soon as the Commodore landed, the drums rolled, the troops at the word of command from Major Zeland [sic][14] presented arms, the bands struck up 'Star Spangled Banner', and gun-

---

[12] To quote from the official source: 'The building had been surrounded by the usual enclosure of cloth, which completely excluded it from the view of those without and in fact seemed to enclose it within a sort of prison yard. . . . The Commodore sent an officer on shore to demand what it meant, and in answer to some frivolous pretext about preventing intrusions and doing honor to the occasion, informed the Japanese that he would forego the honor, and that, until it was completely removed, he could not think of landing. It was immediately taken down by the Japanese.' THE EXPEDITION OF AN AMERICAN SQUADRON. v. 1, p. 344.

[13] Commander Franklin Buchanan (1800–74) in command of the steam frigate *Susquehanna*. On July 14, 1853, when the President's letter was presented to the representatives of the Japanese Government at Uraga, he was the first officer to set foot on Japanese soil.

[14] Major Jacob Zeilen, Marine Corps.

boats commenced saluting. The first salute was a national one of twenty-one guns, and the second a commodore's of seventeen guns, or rather a minister's, for it was in that capacity that the Commodore appeared, being styled by the Japanese the 'Lord High Commissioner from America.'

Preceded by the broad pennant, the pole of which was ornamented with a gilt battle-ax head, and followed by the officers composing the suite [with] six armed negro servants bringing up the rear, the Commodore passed up between the lines bare-headed, and entering the building disappeared from my view (my station being in charge of the boats from this ship).

Being close to the shore and having a good spy-glass, I observed with ease everything that was going on outside. I saw them passing up and down the lines with cake and candy for the officers, who also made them distribute it among the sailors and soldiers. The two bands of music performed alternately, relieved by a strong muster of drums and fifes. The latter excited their curiosity very much, it being a kind of music which they could better understand. The open space included about five acres, round which were erected canvas screens like their flags, with white, black, and white stripes and diamond-shaped holes out at regular intervals. Here and there for some extent a cord only [sic] denoted the line of demarkation,[15] and here were assembled crowds of natives, most of them being servants, evidently, from their liveries. Some were of blue with white stripes of different shapes, others of a reddish colour with lacquered hats on, shaped or formed like those of the Chinese. Numbers of the outsiders would watch their opportunity and creep in to see the show, when the Japanese authorities, observing them, would attempt to seize them; and the race that ensued reminded me of a miltia training when the police officers are in chase of boys.

Referring to the drawing: on the right are a company of archers and matchlock men, being part of the bodyguard of Counselor Linn,[16] the Japanese negotiator. I frequently directed my glass toward them, and for upwards of three hours I saw no perceptible change of position, but all were like so many statues. How long they had been stationed there before our arrival, I can't say, but the attentive observation of

[15] The author meant that merely a small section was enclosed with canvas screens, while the rest was marked off only with a rope.

[16] Linn is the Chinese reading of the Japanese name Hayashi, the chief commissioner. Sproston evidently got the pronunciation from a Chinese interpreter.

orders on the part of soldiers, servants, boatmen, and all other retainers shows the perfect subjugation in which they are kept by their rulers. Their bows were beautiful specimens of archery, about eight feet in length, bowed at each end but straight in the middle. To this straight part is attached the quiver which is lacquered. The cord is of catgut. I will give a drawing of both matchlock and bow when opportunity admits of a closer inspection. Their hats were also highly lacquered and of the Chinese form.

On the left hand, but beyond the limits of the drawing, were congregated a large crowd of curious observers deeply interested in the, to them, novel proceedings of the day. These distributed among the officers bunches of flowers. The variety was not great, but single wild Japonicas were numerous. Some of the officers mingled among them singly, being desirous of examining their swords and garments. At first they showed a disinclination to draw the former, which the officers seeing they immediately drew their own and presented them for inspection. This caused the act to be reciprocated on their part. The guard having stacked arms, were now roaming about at will foremost among the observed and the observing.

It being about one p.m., I sent a boat ashore with the grog to freshen their nip. In the meantime negotiations had commenced. The Commodore, attended by five officers and the Japanese Commissioner, followed by a like number, had retired to a private room to arrange preliminaries, whilst the remainder of the suite in the company of several princes and the Governor of Uraga[17] (the place of the former conference) occupied the main building discussing a rather limited bill of fare, the principal viands being cold soup sweetened, snake chowder,[18] mixed vegetables, cake and candy. Not being as yet able to speak from personal observation of the interior of the building, I shall not at present give any description of it.

About half past three p.m., the drum sounded to quarters [and] officers and men resumed their stations. About a dozen Japanese conveyed a number of kegs and boxes containing *sake* and sweetmeats down to the landing (presents to the Commodore). A few minutes after, several Japanese authorities passed along the line and entered their boats; these were followed in time by the Commodore, accompanied by the Commissioner and the two suites. Again the drums rolled, the escort presented arms, the bands sounded their martial

---

[17] Ezaimon Kayama.   [18] Not snake, but probably fish, chowder.

1 *House of Reception in Kanagawa*

strains. When the barge pulled from the landing, the men in the boats rose and doffed their cap [s], the officers saluted, then the boats were beached. The seamen, marines, bandmen, having again been martialed in their respective boats, and the line abreast reformed, the escort set out on its return in good order, and all expressed themselves well satisfied with the proceedings of the day.

On the following day, Captain Adams, fleet captain, met a deputation of the Japanese[19] on board the *Mississippi* and held a consultation. This was followed by several similar interviews.

At last the day was appointed for the landing and presentation of the presents, and our worthy Captain, as second in rank, was chosen to deliver them; and, fortunately for me, I was ordered by him to act as aide, which fully coincided with my inclinations. The day previous to the ceremony, I conveyed to each captain a schedule of the proceedings 'in expectant'.

MARCH 13TH

THE morning unexpectedly proved to be a cloudy one, and in the course of the day it commenced raining. The launches, however, being filled with boxes, and everything in state of preparation, the Captain concluded it would be better to carry out the contemplated ceremonies. The boats were in the following order: Captain Lee[20] leading in his gig; a line of boats abreast, some of them containing the presents, kept position about a ship's length astern; and our gig, steered by myself, brought up the rear.

On reaching the landing, the marine guard and band were drawn up in line, the former numbering sixty, privates and non-commissioned officers included. When the Captain, followed by myself as aide passed, the guard presented arms, and the band struck up the 'Star Spangled Banner'. The officers then entered the building and seated themselves according to rank.

This being the first time that I had seen the interior of the building, I will give a description of its general appearance. The main room of reception was, I should think, about sixty by fifty feet, and covered with white matting. On each side were ranged two tiers of seats

---

[19] On March 9th, Kahei Kurokawa and his interpreter, Einosuke Moriyama, came to deliver a copy of the proceedings of the day before and its Dutch translation.

[20] Commander S.S. Lee of the *Mississippi*.

covered with thick cloth and silks figured, without backs, but other-wise comfortable.

The upper end of the room was screened off by curtains of silk with the arms of the Emperor[21] upon them. Having, as I said, seated our-selves, we were informed by the interpreter that four of the principal men[22] of the Kingdom were waiting to receive the Captain and his im-mediate suite, or rather they were sitting opposite at the time, but would retire to the other apartment with the Captain—Captains Abbott [sic][23] and Adams, myself, Mr. Perry[24] as reporter, Mr. Portman[25] (interpreter), and Mr. Abbott [sic],[26] and Mr. Williams.[27]

The room that we were ushered into was oblong and small. Seats ranged on three sides covered with red cloth, with low, narrow tables in front with figured silk covers. The Japanese Commissioner and associates seated themselves opposite to us. I then rose and handed two documents to the Captain, who, seated, handed them to the interpreter, Mr. Portman, who passed them to the Japanese inter-preter (he kneeling and bowing down during the whole interview). He delivered them to the Commissioner, in a prostrate position, with the message, which stated they contained a list of the articles and a desire of their acceptance. The reply was delivered through the same channel, returning thanks and accepting them in the name of the Emperor.

'Tis a rough sketch of the presentation in the private audience room. First is Mr. Portman, interpreter, then Captain Abbott, next to him Captain Adams, then the Captain's son, and the last or nearest one, young Perry, taking notes.[28] The Japanese interpreter is seated on the floor.

The Japanese authorities, four in number, are on the left.

After a mutual exchange of friendly sentiments, they retired to frame some documents relative to a final interview with the Com-modore and we were served with refreshments. First, tea was handed round, the cups of China on lacquered stands with globular lacquered

---

[21] Not the crest of the Emperor, but that of the Shogun Tokugawa which consists of three stylized leaves of hollyhock.

[22] They were Ki Hayashi (1799–1858), rector of the University; Satohiro Ido (*d.* 1858), lord of Tsushima; Masayoshi Izawa, lord of Mimasaku; Nagatoshi Udono (1808–69), member of the Board of Revenue.

[23] Captain Joel Abbot (1793–1855) com-manding the *Macedonian.*

[24] Oliver Hazard Perry, third son of Com-modore Perry, who accompanied him as his secretary. After he resigned from the Navy, he was United States Consul in Hongkong, and died in London May 17, 1870.

[25] A. L. C. Portman, Commodore's clerk and interpreter.

[26] Joseph Abbot, son of Captain Abbot, who acted as his clerk.

[27] Samuel Wells Williams (1812–84), chief interpreter.

[28] N. B. Adams, son of Captain Henry A. Adams, who acted as his clerk.

2 *Private Audience Room*

tops. In a few minutes that was followed by a service of handsomely gilt and lacquered ware consisting of plates, saucers with covered cups containing boiled fish, stewed venison and chicken, omelette, and vegetables cooked with sugar, and to complete this *dejeuner, à la batons de rice*, preserves tasting like fig paste, and guava jelly after.[29] They handed also to each one a small china plate of salt, which is an article never used by them, but it being the first fresh meal that I had enjoyed for some time, dispensed with it myself. Having finished our repast, such as desired and, what was more to the purpose, had them, regaled themselves with a cigar.

In obedience to the instructions of the Captain, I informed the officers in the main room who were enjoying a less *recherché* repast, that when they had finshed, the room would be cleared for the reception of the presents which had been by this time drawn up, large and small, to the outer building.

In the course of half an hour the boxes containing the articles for the Emperor[30] and second officer of the Empire (who, by the by, was this very counselor officiating) and some other officials, being open, and the contents of a few, principally swords and firearms, being exposed to view, the Captain, in the presence of his officers, and through the usual course of verbal communication, delivered over the presents to the Japanese princes who represented the Emperor.

The pith of his very appropriate address was to this effect: In selecting these presents our Government has had in view utility moer than richness. We could have made a more rich, not a more useful, display. They are consequently suited to use—not to show—and as such we would have you consider them.

He continued to say that of the more valuable, there we[re] duplicates and triplicates that would be sent on shore in a day or two, and that the machinery and engine and also magnetic telegraph would be put up and got into operation as soon as possible. To this the second Commissioner or third man of the Kingdom (who had been deputed by the first to receive them), made an appropriate reply.[31]

The ceremony being over, we were prevented by the inclemency of the weather from walking in the country, as we had originally in-

---

[29] Japanese candy called *yōkan* made of bean paste.

[30] Not knowing the military regime of feudal Japan, the members of the American expedition confused the Shogun who dwelled in Yedo with the Emperor who was in Kyōto. Any future reference to the Emperor should be considered as the Shogun, unless otherwise noted.

[31] Satohiro Ido, lord of Tsushima.

tended; so that a few minutes after, we were pulling back to the ship, followed by the escort of boats.

Of the kind and quality of the presents, I shall make no mention at present, hoping, as I do, in three or four days to see them displayed to better advantage and the scientific portion in operation.

Again an interview has taken place between the Commodore and the Japanese,[32] the result of which is not known; but the fact of the *Vandalia* and *Southampton* having gone down to survey the harbour of a large town[33] foreshadows the truth of the report that three Japanese cities[34] will be opened for our commercial purposes.

Most of the presents had been sent up to Yedo. The locomotive and miniature car yet remained. The telegraph wires also stretched along as far as the eye could see. And a large country wagon and cart stood on the open space. I suppose that they could only be transported by water.

I had charge of the gunboat today, but was politely relieved by an officer so that I had an opportunity of seeing what was going on in the main room. The officers were partaking of a slight repast and drinking tea and smoking. The Commodore was in his council room, and great numbers of Japanese officials and attendants were sitting near-by.

In the morning we had noticed from the ship that a very beautiful looking barge was being towed by several boats fantastically fitted up.[35] The barge was very gaudily painted and had numerous flags and streamers flying from flagpoles both forward and at the tafferel.

When anchored off the shore, I had an excellent opportunity of observing this, as it proved to be a prince's barge. It appears that a young prince gifted with considerable curiosity had come down from Yedo to have a view of the squadron, but not to participate in the day's

---

[32] To quote Samuel Wells Williams: 'FRIDAY, MARCH 17TH.—The Commodore left the ship to-day at one o'clock, and was received on shore by the marines and an escort, with music and met the four commissioners in the house. The confernce was altogether about three hours and a half, and conducted very pleasantly by the Japanese. The refusal to go to Nagasaki at all was met by the proposal of another port, when Perry mentioned Uraga, and they Shimoda, pointing it out on the map. This place had a fine harbor, and the Commodore agreed to it provisionally, saying that he must first examine its location, and would send the 'Vandalia' and 'Southampton' down there immediately to inspect and survey it.'

'A Journal of the Perry Expedition to Japan.' TRANSACTIONS OF THE ASIATIC SOCIETY OF JAPAN. xxxvii: part 2; 1910; p. 140.

[33] Shimoda.

[34] Shimoda and Hakodate, only two cities, were opened by the Treaty of Kanagawa for American ships to obtain wood, water, coal and provisions, as well as other necessities.

[35] The *Tenchi-maru*, one of the official barges of the Shogun, built in the 18th century and reconditioned in 1831. She was 165 feet in length and 57 feet in breadth, and was well equipped for an extended voyage. This day a few members of the Tokugawa family and high officials of the Shogunate came down from Kanagawa to see the squadron.

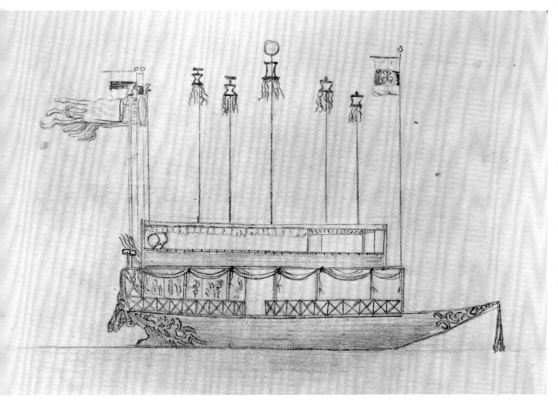

3 Official Barge of the Shōgun

ceremonies. I did not see him myself, but was told that he was not more than twenty-four years of age.

The barge was about fifty feet in length by twenty in breadth[36] and had two decks. She was painted red elaborately gilded, the bow and counter being ornamented with copper cut into the form of dragons or tendrils. The upper deck was covered by an awning of red and white striped cotton, and sides hung with silk curtains, those festooned round the lower deck being of ma[roon] coloured silk, evidently the colour peculiar to his house. The flags were of several kinds. One kind was attached to hoops suspended from the flagpoles and terminating in a number of strips or tails, very much like a piece of white paper cut and fitted round a candle stick. Then there was the imperial flag, two aft, one forward, of white, black, and white stripes, with a white ○ in the black stripe, and three hearts pointing toward each other in that.[37] The prince's fiag was the midship flag, astern, of white, maroon, and white stripes, a white in the maroon stripe.

MARCH 23RD

ONCE more did a visit of ceremony take place between the Commodore and Commissioners. I went in charge of our boats, but without the howitzer. The men, however, were armed as usual. I had also another officer with me, who remained by the boat after the marines were landed, thereby enabling me to see the proceedings of the morning.

In the principal audience hall were displayed the presents from the Emperor of Japan to our Government. As I entered, the Commodore and Commissioners passed out to the open space in front where seats were ranged for their convenience, but for what I did not then know. Without dealy, I entered the building and being at the time the only inmate of the room, had an excellent opportunity of closely examining the various articles spread out before me, of which I will now give a description.

The first objects that attracted my attention were the lacquered boxes of different sizes and shapes, embracing several varieties of style, [the] exterior of some being plain, the interior dark purple with gilding. Others had on the exterior raised metal figures of birds, some six inches in length and beautifully executed, also vines and

---

[36] Sproston was mistaken about the size of the barge.

[37] They were not hearts, but three stylized hollyhock leaves in a circle, the crest of the Tokugawa family.

flowers. Besides boxes, there were sets of small drawers supported in a stand, resembling a miniature wardrobe without doors in front. These were also gilt.

Then there were several low tables exactly like (in form, not material) tables I had often seen used at Loo Choo by the scribes, to write upon—they sitting cross-legged by them.[38] These were ornamentad like the boxes, excepting that the figures were not raised. Covered cups, plates, saucers, cup stands, and chow-chow stands, completed the assortment of lacquer-ware, as well as I remember. Their quality was evidently very superior and beautiful, evidently excelling every other nation. For instance as ocular demonstration, I compared several articles of Chinese lacquer-ware with some procured at Loo Choo and found the former very inferior to the latter, which in its turn could be compared with a similar kind here displayed. Of the more beautiful varieties, no other nation can produce them.

The silk and crape department next attracted my attention. Both were of pat[tern] very similar to our own. The former wanted body, but the latter was very superior in style and texture. Besides the abovementioned articles there were many others, some of which were packed up so that I could not discover what they were. Returning to the open space in front of the building, I found the officers and Japanese assembled witnessing the marine guard drill, which they did very well. The manoeuvering evidently astonished them.

The marine drill over, the Chief Commissioner waved his fan and gave an order, when immediately some 25 or 30, for [the] Japanese, large, powerful, and stout men, robed only in waist cloths, came forward, and at the word of command each seized from a large pile two bags of rice, each weighing from 160 to 180 pounds, and carrying them a distance of about three hundred feet, piled them up again. Then two or three of the stoutest, taking one of the bags and raising it up above his head, threw it up, and, turning it at the same time, caught it at the other end. [An]other, again, raising it breast high, would turn a somersault lifting it with him as he rose again. The rice was then presented to the Commodore, who sent it off in the launches.

We then adjourned to the Treaty House. The paper-covered windows on one side had been drawn aside and seats arranged for the officers near-by. The ground in front had been cleaned and a ring

---

[38] According to the memorandum of the Commissioners, dated March 13, these were individual dinner tables used at Japanese banquets.

...three of the crowd, taking one of the bags and raising
it up above his head threw it up and turning it at the
same time caught it at the other end. Others again raising
it breast high would turn a somerset lifting it with him
as he rose again.

4 *Japanese Wrestlers*

The rice was then presented to the Commodore who sent it
off in the launches. We then adjourned to the Treaty House, the

formed. A Japanese official then took his station at one end and called off the wrestlers by pairs, who appeared upon the arena two at a time. After each round, they took a mouthful of *sake* and rubbed some salt upon their breasts.[39] They first assembled together round the ring and went through a rather classical or gladiatorial pantomime, in which their large proportions appeared to advantage. They then retired, and the first two were called out. They took positions at opposite ends of the ring, and in a stooping position clasped their hands twice before them, then spread out their arms full length, after which they advanced into the middle of the ring and stretched their limbs, then stooping down with a short, sharp cry, they closed in the contest. Their method of wrestling differed from our own in not using their feet, but confining their exertions to the muscular use of their hands and arms and butting with the head upon the chests and shoulders. In their respirations they would give forth a sound like 'Hiss-hiss'; others reminded me very much of the words, 'Yes Sir' or as they pronounced it, 'Yes Sa'.[40]

When one of the combatants would be thrown or forced out of the ring, he would either return to the contests and make one or more efforts to overcome his opponent, or, bowing his head as he assumed a half-stooping position, would thus acknowledge his defeat.

This exhibition over, we sat down to a chow-chow at which I demolished four or five dozen oysters with a splinter of wood[41] for a fork, also eggs, fish, cake, and candy, and carried off, like the rest, the remnants of the feast in a piece of paper. We then returned to the boats, re-embarked with the presents, and reached our ships in a half-gale of wind.

MARCH 28TH

THIS day clear with a strong northerly wind. Put our ship in prime order, and dressed the crew in white frocks over blue. At 2 p.m. the Japanese boats were seen approaching from the direction of the town. Three stopped at the *Mississippi*, whilst the fourth, containing the interpreter, pulled to our ship, and he told us in very good English that the Commissioners requested that Captain Adams might be sent for to accompany them in their visits to the different ships, they being,

---

[39] As a part of their ritual, the wrestlers purge themselves with salt before they enter the sanded ring.

[40] *Yassa, yassa* is a kind of Japanese yell.
[41] Sproston probably means a pair of chopsticks.

I suppose, more accustomed to him than [to] other officers, [since] as flag captain he had had considerable intercourse with them.

The Commissioners having walked round the decks of the *Mississippi*, took their departure for our ship, and the officers assembled on the quarter-deck to receive them. The boats with the retainers first came alongside. They, assembling on each side of the gangway and bowing to the Commissioners on their hands and knees as they passed them, followed on behind. The boatswain piped and the marine guard presented arms. The Captain introduced the officers and then walked them round the spar-deck, showing them the large ten-inch pivot guns, being larger guns than they ever saw before; but they betrayed very little astonishment. Then they visited the cabin and officers' apartments, gun and berth decks, and all the other parts of the ship, with which they were very much pleased.

We went to general quarters, exercised the big guns, called away boarders, pikemen, firemen, axemen, carbineers, and pumpmen, going through the various evolutions with a great deal of spirit, and having evidently the desired effect upon them of convincing them of our power and force when occasion required.

The exercise being over, the Commissioners shoved off in their boats for the *Powhatan* where they were to be entertained in a more substantial manner. Five or six officers from this ship, I among the number, then started in a boat for the flag-ship which we found handsomely decorated with flags, and on the quarter-deck were ranged tables, or I might say a table, for they were placed so as to form one continuous display of delicacies, many of which I, for one, had not seen or partaken of for months.

The Commissioners had been examining the machinery, they having steam up and slowly revolving the wheels to show them the operation of the several parts of massive iron jointed together. What knowledge they possess of steam I cannot say, but I am told that the interpreter understands well the principal and motive power, and I should judge from their intercourse with the Dutch that they had informed themselves of the various discoveries in science, mechanism, made heretofore by enlightened nations.

Having walked round the ship, they descended into the cabin with the Commodore and captains, where they were no doubt well entertained. Their retainers remained on deck and joined us in the onslaught upon the numerous edibles there displayed. Champagne, sherry, port, whisky, punch, and, in fact, every kind and quality of wine or liquor

5 *American Squadron in Shimoda: 'The above is a rough outline
of our position at meridian.'*

they came first to hand, satisfied their wants. A rather tall and gaunt Japanese that sat next to me drank them all, and was, of course, rather merry afterwards.

The various toasts of the evening were: 'Japan and California— may they be united by steam and commerce'; 'The Emperor and Empress of Japan'; 'The ladies of Japan—may we become better acquainted with them'. And most heartily did I echo that sentiment, for I have become tired of looking at nothing but men month after month. 'The ladies of America'—the above was re-echoed in my mind. Japanese pipes and cheroots now made their appearance, and a sociable smoke followed, the band performing some of their best airs.

In the course of the afternoon the Commodore made his appearance on deck with the Commissioners and said, 'Gentlemen, we will now adjourn to hear the minstrels.' A profound silence succeeded this an-[nouncement] which was succeeded by a shrill whistle from one of the Japanese, which caused considerable excitement and laughter. The Commodore looked grave (no one appreciates a joke less than he does). However, all hands proceeded to the place of amusement in anticipation, some finding an elevated position on the top of the cabin to enjoy the scene the Japanese being placed in front. The Commodore, captains, and Commissioners seating themselves, the performance commenced.

When the sable gentlemen made their appearance, a murmur of astonishment arose among our simple guests. Woolly heads, standing shirt collars of ample dimensions, and black faces, contrasting with black and yellow striped coats, ruffled shirts, and the usual p[ants] of a darky band were truly new sights to them. 'Yah-Yah-Sambo, how you be?' said Bones to Tambourine, as the one rattled and the other knocked his instrument in their faces. I thought the Commissioners would have died with their suppressed laughter (for they never laughed out as we do). The dancing rather surpassed all, and during this part of the performance, I looked, and to my astonishment, saw an arm placed affectionately round the Commodore's neck. That arm appertained to the Chief Commissioner.[42] What will not champagne do! And thus closed the day's amusement.

---

[42] That arm did not belong to Commissioner Hayashi, but to Mantaro Matsuzaki (*d.* 1854) who was his secretary. Matsuzaki was a Confucian scholar of Yedo and recognized for his brilliance. His long figure and yellow bilious face together with his excessive shortsightedness, however, did not make a pleasing impression on the Americans. Following the Oriental tradition of scholars, Matsuzaki was fond of alcoholic beverages and*

MARCH 31ST

THIS day has the treaty of amity and friendship been signed by the Commodore and Commissioners. Captain Adams sails with it for the United States in a day or two, taking passage as far as the Sand[wich] Islands in the *Saratoga*.

MARCH——[43]

THE *Saratoga* set sail this morning and was cheered by the whole squadron as she stood out of the harbour, homeward bound. May prosperous winds attened her! Still she has half the world and stormy Cape Horn to encompass before she reaches her wished-for haven of rest and security.

APRIL 11TH

IN obedience to signal from the flag-ship, the squadron this morning got under way, the steamers leading, and stood out of the harbour of Kanagawa, bound we hardly knew whither. When about three miles from our former anchorage, we noticed that the *Lexington* was aground. The Commodore sent the *Vandalia's* launch to her assistance. When we had reached the middle of the Bay, signal was made and the squadron anchored. We had felt considerable curiosity as to whether we would go to Yedo or not, and the general opinion was that the Commodore intended to anchor as close to the Capital of Japan as he could; and the fact of the wind being from the northeast, which was ahead, accounted for our anchoring without changing our destination.

But in the course of an hour or so we were again under way and standing down the harbour, anchored off Webster Island, or, in other words, came to in the American Anchorage. Naturally curious as to the reason of our apparently uncertain movements during the day, I enquired for an explanation form some of the officers of the flag-ship and received the following solution:

It was well known to all that the Commodore on the day the treaty

---

*showed at the banquet on board the *Powhatan* a decided appreciation of the champagne and other wines. Upon leaving, the excited scholar threw his arms about the Commodore's neck and repeated again and again, 'Nippon and America all same heart,' in Japanese.

[43] This is Sproston's error. The *Saratoga* set sail on April 4th.

was signed expressed to the Commissioners his intention of visiting
Yedo. But they dissented, saying they had not the power to grant him
the privilege, having no instruction on that point, and politely declined
the offer of a passage in the steamers. The Commodore, however,
reiterated to them his intention of doing so. The next day we heard
of the interpreters having said that if the Commodore went up to Yedo,
they would commit the *H[arakiri]* (bellycut).

Now the steamers had, when first under way, headed up the Bay in
the direction of a pagoda on a small island which we called Yedo
Beacon,[44] but that afterwards they had changed their course. The two
Japanese boats towing astern convinced us that the interpreters were
on board. From what we could learn, it appears that the one on board
of the *Mississippi* actually became sick when he saw the course of the
steamers, and when they [were] only a few miles from Yedo, commenced standing right up in the direction of that port. He threw his
cloak and long sword to young Speiden[45] saying, 'Take them, for I
have no more need of them. My short sword will be all that I shall
require.'[46]

APRIL 18TH

WE have now been at sea six days, having sailed the morning following our anchorage off Webster Island, bound to the Bonin Islands.[47] We stood down the Bay of Yedo with steering sails set on
both sides, and this time passed to the eastward of [the main island],

[44] The pagoda of the Kawasaki Daishi, a
famous shrine, at Kawasaki.

[45] Lieutenant William Speiden (*d.* 1861).

[46] After the treaty was signed, the Commodore said that the President ordered him to go
to Yedo and that he was going. The Japanese
officials explained that they failed to obtain the
consent of the Shogun. And entreated and
begged him not to go. To quote Samuel Wells
Williams:

'. . . .As we (Americans) had professed
friendly feelings for them, they wished us as
friends not to go, and would regard it as a
personal favor, and, lastly, that very serious
personal consequences might result, intimat-
ing almost jeopardy of honor and life, if we
thus implicated them.'

Commodore Perry, however, was determined, and Williams continues: 'We went within
about eight miles of a long row of stakes stretching along in front of Yedo, but not so near as
to prevent large junks lying inside of it, and

turned about in one hundred feet of water! If
a man is a commodore, I suppose he can do as
nobody else would, in order to show that he
can do as he likes; and after all that had been
said about going to Yedo, to say that we had
left off four miles short of the surveying boats,
and fully eight of the city, was rather an im-
putation on common sense on our part. . . . I
have upheld and approved the Commodore's
acts in most cases, where others have sharply
ridiculed them, but this day's work was small
enough,' 'A Journal of the Perry Expedition
to Japan.' TRANSACTIONS OF THE ASIATIC
SOCIETY OF JAPAN. V. XXXVII: part 2; 1910;
pp. 160-162.

[47] Ogasawara-jima form a group of 27
small islands. The term 'Bonin' is a corruption
of the Japanese 'munin' meaning 'empty of
men,' but the Japanese call them Ogasawara-
jima after Ogasawara, their first discoverer,
in 1593.

which is preferable both going and coming, as you have more sea-room in case of a gale springing up. The first three days out we experienced rainy, blowy weather, wind generally from the northeast. The weather being continually overcast, we were unable to determine our position every day, which was very much to be desired, as there is a regular gulf stream or strong current sweeping along the coast of Japan, of which but little is known.

The *Saratoga*, when near the entrance to Yedo Bay, was swept to the northward and eastward and was three weeks [days?] working back. We experienced a heavy tumbling sea which made everyone seasick, at all predisposed that way. The air and water, taken every hour, differed from six to ten degrees, the water being the warmer, and in every respect the appearances were the same as we would have encountered in our own Gulf Stream, excepting in this case there was no gulfweed. This boisterous weather was succeeded by a calm which lasted twenty-four hours, but it was warm, pleasant weather, such as I remembered having enjoyed a long time ago, and greeted its return with an equal warmth of feeling.

We had so far passed near to, but not in sight of, any of the numerous islands which abound in these seas, contrary winds having prevented us from doing so. They are all small and uninhabited, but, as seldom any vessels but whalers visit these waters, the position of many of these islands as laid down on the chart must be incorrect; it is very necessary that any such mistake should be corrected, as in all probability before many years, hundreds of ships will pass through these groups in the California and China trade.

On the 15th we made St. Peter's Island,[48] but to windward and distant about fifteen miles. It appeared to be a small little conical island, and looked very solitary, standing alone by itself. Bearing up, we shaped our course for another island[49] without a name, distant fifty miles; but we could not discover it. On the 16th we experienced a night of wind and rain which caused a considerable sea to rise. On the morning of the 17th I had the morning watch, and shortly after I came on deck, the wind hauled so that the ship lay her course, but it still blew in heavy squalls with blinding showers of rain. Ship under-reefed courses and treble-reefed topsails, commenced pitching heavily into the sea, which was now head on, so as to bury the bowsprit most every

---

[48] Or better known as Ponafiden Island— Tori-jima in Japanese.

[49] Smith Island or Sumisu-jima.

plung[e], and thoroughly wet anyone who attempted to go forward of the foremast.

With the exception of a few squalls of rain, the day proved pleasant. In the afternoon two sails were reported in sight from aloft, which, on nearing them, proved to be whalers, both hoisting American colours, one a ship and the other a barque. The barque passed close to us and hove to. We did the same, and the first mate came alongside in a whale-boat, which, impelled by four long oars and steered by a fifth, fairly danced over the long heaving swell. He stated the barque to be the *Rambler*,[50] six days out from the Bonins where they had been provisioning ship. He said they were two years and a half out from the United States and had five hundred barrels of sperm; they were then bound to the Japan Seas. We informed him of the existing treaty between the two countries and pointed out the commercial ports on the chart which were open to us. Our ship having only one or two servings of lamp oil left on board, we took advantage of the opportunity to purchase a barrel of sperm.

The mate reported the ship to windward to be the American whale-ship *Roscoe*,[51] also, I believe, from Nantucket, with fourteen hundred barrels of sperm oil, and forty eight months out from the United States. This ship was formerly a New York packet and a fine vessel. She sailed for England the same day we sailed from New York, bound to Gibralter, in the *Lexington*. This was in '43. In '48 when on the Brazil station, I boarded her when she came into Rio as a trader with a cargo of flour, and now, in '54, I meet her again in the Japan Seas as a whaler. She was so near that without the aid of a glass we could discern her three lookouts perched in their crow's nests aloft, looking out upon the vast expanse of water beneath them, patiently awaiting the wished-for sight of 'There she spouts!'

And this is the whaler's life month after month, occasionally putting into some inhabited island for provision, and then out to sea again, and when their cruising ground is regained, drifting along under easy sail. Day after day passes in one monotonous round, varied only by the occasional exciting capture of a whale, and the consequent process which follows, of disposing of this leviathan of the deep in the most lucrative manner. Can there be imagined a more unintellectual life than this! And yet with them, life has its objects as it

---

[50] The *Rambler* of New Bedford, under Captain James M. Willis, sailed on October 4, 1852, and returned on June 10, 1856.

[51] The *Roscoe* of New Bedford, under Captain A. Robeson, sailed on August 4, 1851, and returned on April 8, 1855.

has with all men. Well for society is it that the objects of men and their modes of accomplishing them differ so greatly.

A few minutes before parting company with the *Rambler*, another sail was reported from aloft, and soon became vis[ible] from the deck. She was evidently a whaler, but her course being opposite and par-[allel] to our own, we did not speak her. The *Mary and Elizabeth*,[52] no doubt, a whaler provisioning at Bonin when the *Rambler* left. She had been out four years.

The night was very squally; and the first part of the morning, light airs and misty weather. The wind has not been blowing from the west for three days past; that is, since the calm that followed the heavy north-east gales we experienced on our first departure from Japan, and we are all very anxious to get in and enjoy a little exercise, of which we stand very much in need.

Made another American whaler today, which I boarded. She proved to be the *Mildon* [sic][53] of New Bedford, fourteen hundred barrels, and thirty months out.

He—that is, Captain Jones—had left Bonin a day and a half ago only, and presenting me with some fresh Provisions, which were very acceptable, accompanied me back to the ship in his shirt sleeves and a slouch hat.

We procured from the *Mildon* two barrels of oil; were so pure as to be almost tasteless. Tobacco, papers and the like were given to the captain, including a paper of smoking tabacco from myself, which he prized very much. Cruising beyond the bounds of civilization, they have but few opportunities of procuring those little comforts which compensate in a measure for the many necessary deprivations attending a life on shipboard.

In the meantime, a southwest wind had sprung up, so that when we lay our course S.S.E. and were obliged to shorten sail so as not to average over eight miles an hour—the Bonins being only distant ninety miles, and the night proved dark and squally with rain at intervals. I may here remark, what no doubt has often been mentioned before, that in the neighorhood of islands you always experience similar weather, more or less, according to the season of the year. It is

[52] The *Mary and Elizabeth* does not appear in the list of whaling vessels of the Commissioner of Fish and Fisheries, and all the other contemporary sources I have gone through failed to identify this ship. However, according to the log of the *Macedonian*, the *Margaret Scott* is reported, and probably Sproston is referring to her. She was of New Bedford, and under Captain B.C. Eldridge, sailed on May 21, 1851, and returned on May 6, 1855.

[53] The *Milton*, under Captain Silas Jones, sailed on August 18 1851, and returned in 1854.

a natural consequence readily accounted for on philosophical [sic] principles, and which in connection with tides and currents marks the navigation of such very precarious, especially at night, when their influences upon the ship canot be ascertained, and more particurly in these seas when the charts are often incorrect or at least imperfect. The positions of many of the islands here are so doubtful, in fact their actual existence so uncertain, that they have not received a name.

APRIL 18TH

AT daylight made a group of islands on our lee bow and bore up for them, but on our nearer approach we discovered that they were the northern part of the Bonins called the Parry Group[54] (named after the celebrated arctic navigator of that name). We immediately hauled our wind, but it proved too late. We could not head our course, and were obliged to go about and stand off on the opposite tack to gain an offing. In doing so we sailed along the group, which, as far as we could judge, consisted of four islands in a line, of volcanic origin (I never saw an island that was not); but the most singular thing that met our view was the fact that numerous large holes could be seen extending through their bases, worn there, no doubt, by the continual action of the waves. Two were low and flat on top, but the other two presented a peaked, jagged front, with but little vegetation upon their surfaces. Off the most easterly, we discovered a coral reef extending perhaps over two miles out to sea and not noted on the chart.

The afternoon has been clear and pleasant; wind light from the southward. Peel Island,[55] in which is situated Port Lloyd,[56] and to which we are bound, is in sight to windward, distant about twenty miles. We have shortened sail, and will stand off and on during the first part of the night, and make sail again before daylight with the reasonable hope of getting in tomorrow and enjoying our longed-for run on shore.

APRIL 19TH

TAKING the deck in the mid-watch, I found the ship under topsails on the offshore tack. The moon shown [sic] dimly through the passing clouds, and the light wind occasionally freshening, a light shower of

---

[54] Mukojima Retto.   [55] Chichi-jima.   [56] Futami-kō.

rain would follow, but in a few minutes it would pass over, and, the breeze subsiding, the sails would again flap listless[ly] against the masts. The watch, having picked out the softest planks they could find, wrapped themselves in their peajackets for protection from the occasional showers [and] were soon in a profound sleep.

Not a sound broke the stillness of the night, except the occasional creaking of a block or the call of the lookouts when the half-hour bell struck. The ship rose and fell on the long swell, and the waves rippled audibly under the bows. Heavy masses of clouds were dotted along the horizon to leeward, indicating the position of the several islands composing the Parry Group. To windward Peel Island could be dimly seen through the night glass, its dark sides rendered still more dark by the flickering rays of the moon. The repose of all surrounding objects was catching. I walked the deck smartly to keep my faculties awake. In the midst of a profound meditation on the comparative merits of cruising among civilized and savage people—that is, deprivations—I was interrupted by the master's coming on deck and saying, 'Make sail.'

Rousing up the watch, I made sail to Royals and T—lying Lib. Shortly afterwards, the wind heading us off, went about; but being headed again, tacked ship a second time. Strike eight bells. 'Call the watch' soon followed this last manoeuver, and I turned the deck over to Watters,[57] who passed the next four hours in bracing the yards to a wind that changed, as he afterwards expressed it, in both force and direction rather faster than the sails could be trimmed.

And as a climax it rained hard the whole watch, thoroughly wetting him through. During the forenoon and most of the afternoon it blew a fresh topgallant breeze with heavy rain squalls, but the evening proved clear and pleasant. At sunset we had worked up into a position, which, if we hold it during the night, will enable us to get into port early in the morning, not being distant more than four miles.

MORNING OF THE 20TH

To our astonishment the master found during the mid-watch by an observation of the North Star that we were to the southward of Peel Island some forty miles, and that we had been doing our best the day previous to make the best of our way from our port of destination.

---

[57] Lieutenant John Watters (*d.* 1874).

This was, to say the least, very aggravating, but when once the discovery was made, we could readily account for it in this wise.

In the first place, we ran down to Parry Group supposing it to be main group. Finding such not to be the case, we hauled our wind and commenced beating to the southward, but the wind being light and a lee tide setting us down upon the islands to leeward, we were obliged to stand out to sea. At sunset, the haze along the horizon lifting, we discovered Peel Island to windward, distant about thirty miles bearing S.E. by E. Kept under easy sail most of the night, and stood in for the land at early daylight, and continued tacking off and on during the day, which was squally and rainy so that we could not get an observation; and it was from this cause that we did not discover that during the night we had been set to windward twenty miles so as to be off the Baily Group[58] in the morning, the most southerly of the Bonins.

We had the satisfaction, however, of being to windward of our port and immediately setting our port steering sails, kept away with flowing sheets, a spanking breeze following. At meridian, the largest and most northerly of the Baily Group bore on our lee quarter, whilst Peel Island was in sight on the lee bow. At two p.m., being abreast of it, shortened sail, hoisted the Jack at the fore, and fired first one gun and then another.

Presently, from a bay to leeward of the harbour we saw a canoe pulling out towards the ship, which was now hove to. In the meantime, the Captain, fearing he would not be able to obtain a pilot, had manned two boats to [be] placed in charge of Lieutenant P[59] and myself. We were to pull in and take position on each side at the mouth of the harbour, and having sounded round, anchor on two shoals, thereby showing their position. The approach of the canoe, however, changed his determination, and he sent me in a boat to bring off the pilot, there being considerable sea on at the time. Ranging up alongside the canoe, the pilot (an old gary-headed sailor) scrambled into my boat, saying :—

'If we were not two sculls short this would not have been necessary, for my canoe would ride safely in a seaway where your boat would swamp.'

'Should not judge so from appearances,' was my reply, as I glanced at the roughly hollowed-out trunk supported by its outriggers, a form not peculiar to, but existing among, all the Pacific islands. I will take

[58] Hahajima Retto.　　　[59] Lieutenant George Henry Preble (1816–85).

a sketch of one tomorrow. 'Have you ever heard anything of the fate of Matthews[60] and his boat's crew?'

He pointed out to me the part of the island off which they were lost, and replied.

'Not even a piece of the boat have we ever found.'

What a sad fate: An unknown grave, off an island whose very existence is known only to a few! Towed his canoe off to the ship, questioning him on the way about fresh provisions. Found turtle, sweet potatoes, yams, and fish to be all that we might expect to obtain, as they did not go out shooting goats and wild pigs now, on account of the turtle season, the meat of which they salt down in great quantities. Bananas and pineapples were not yet ripe, unfortunately.

Filling away, we entered the harbour, passing numbers of turtle floating on the surface of the water, and anchored in deep water, close in shore. Taking a boat, I landed the pilot on a coral beach near a collection of huts, and brought off four turtle[s], each of which weighed about four hundred pounds, but were shipped over the side in a trice, and lived but a few minutes after. I look forward with pleasure to turtle steaks in the morning. Went ashore again with the seining party. Hauled the seine twice and caught four hundred fish in spite of the coral bottom, after which sat in Mr. Savery's[61] cabin and smoked a cigar. He is an old sailor and the head man on the Island. Besides him were a number of young men and women, their wives, and a number of children—but I will delay further description for the present.

The above is a sketch of the canoe in which the old pilot 'Horten'[62]

---

[60] Master John Matthews was drowned on October 25, 1853, off Peel Island. To quote from a letter of Commander John Kelly, comdᵉʳ. *U.S.S. Plymouth* from off the Peel Island:
'On October 25 Lieut. Matthews requested permission to take the 2nd cutter with fourteen men and proceed to North Island for the purpose of fishing and shooting wild pigeons, stating he would return by dinner time. He left about 8:30 a.m. and stood off under sail about two miles from the island to speak an English schooner than in the offing. . . .
'The gale was terrific, commencing at N.E. and ending at the N.W. You may judge of the strength of the wind, when I inform you, that this ship, with four anchors down, lower yards and topmast struck, dragged completely across the harbour, with the water as smooth as a mill pond.
'On the 27th I dispatched sailing master H.N.T. Arnold in search of the cutter, supposing she had been stove on landing, and that

the crew were on one of the islands and only waited to be released.
'After two days of ineffectual search, he returned. So far not a vestige of the boat or the crew could be discovered.' THE EXPEDITION OF AN AMERICAN SQUADRON. v. 2, pp. 408-9.

[61] Instructions of Commodore Perry to Captain Abbot, April 10, 1854. 'Sir: You will proceed with the United States ship *Macedonian*, under your command to Port Lloyd, Peel Island, one of the Bonin Group, and there examine into the condition of the small settlement established at that place in 1830, and of which Nathaniel Savery, at the time of my visit to the island, was the only surviving white man of the first settlers.' THE EXPEDITION OF AN AMERICAN SQUADRON. v. 2, p. 127.

[62] Report of Captain Abbot to Commodore Perry, May 2, 1854. '. . . .George Horton, a man who belonged to the *Plymouth*, but being sick with the dropsy, and his time being out, by recommendation of the surgeon he was*

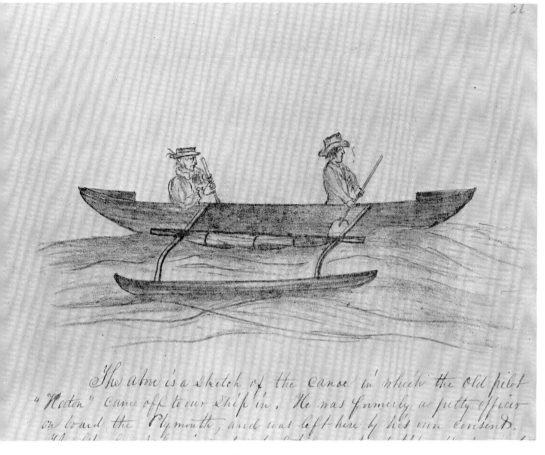

The above is a sketch of the canoe in which the old pilot "Horton" came off to our ship in. He was formerly a petty officer on board the Plymouth, and was left here by his own consent.

6 *Horton's Canoe*

came off to our ship in. He was formerly a petty officer on board the *Plymouth*, and was left here by his own consent. The life of a sailor is made up of toil and hardship afloat and temporary excitement on shore. Enjoying but little ease or comfort in either case, he looks upon the comparatively idle and careless existence of an islander as the beau-ideal of happiness, and it is thus Peel Island has become inhabited.

About thirty two years ago,[63] a schooner flying [British] colours and manned by two American[s],[64] an Englishman,[65] Dane[66] and Italian[67] (singular to say, the latter commanding), with fifteen [natives of the Sandwich Islands], came to this Island in search of seals and sandal-wood; but not finding the one or the other, they gave up their original intention and made a settlement upon the Island.

Savery, the present magistrate, was one of the two Americans. Born in New England near the residence of our Captain, it appears he followed the sea for his fortune, but brought up at last in Lima where he resided six years. From there he went to the Sandwich Islands and joined the party aboard the trading schooner which eventually settled here, where he has since lived, making only occasional visits to China and Manila. The last time he was absent from the Island, nine years ago, a Chinese pirate came into the harbour, seized his wife and a daughter, also four thousand dollars and all his movables. This was told me by his present wife, a [Guamese] woman.[68]

Collins, Webb,[69] and Bravo are the names of three other old settlers. Webb has gone in the Am[erican] whale-ship, *Bowditch*,[70] as first mate, but will return again. Collins has been twenty two years on the Island, his father English, his mother a [Kanaka] woman. His father is now in California and owner of two or three ships. Besides these there are about a dozen sailors, who may or may not remain on the Island, and a few [Kanaka] men.

Sweet potatoes, onions, sugar-cane, turtle[s], hogs goats, and bananas are all they produce at present upon the Island; but by next year they will have several other varieties of vegetables, [because of]

---

*discharged by commander Kelly, and left at Port Lloyd. Since he has been there, he has entirely recovered his health, and has bought a good and comfortable place of a man who desired to leave, and has left the island. Horton, though old, is a smart and serviceable man at the island, and makes an excellent pilot. He piloted the *Macedonian* in and out.' *Ibid*. v. 2, p. 129.

[63] It was in the latter part of 1830.
[64] Nathaniel Savery and Aldin B. Chapin,

both of Massachusetts.
[65] Richard Mildtchamp.
[66] Charles Johnson of Denmark.
[67] Mattheo Mazara of Genoa.
[68] Savery's second wife was the widow of Mattheo Mazara, a native of Guam.
[69] Thomas H. Webb, one of the two councilmen of the island.
[70] The *Bowditch* of Warren, Rhode Island, sailed on August 19, 1852, and returned May 20, 1856.

the seeds given them by Commodore Perry, who at the same time placed a number of sheep and cattle upon adjoining islands. The former are increasing fast, some being Cape sheep, but one of the bulls is dead. They hear the bellow of the cows, but have never seen them as yet.

APRIL 25TH

I had been delaying ever since our arrival for a favourable opportunity to explore the Island, and this morning young Adams and myself started with the intention of making the best of our time, prepared to encounter and overcome all difficulties in our path. Landing on the beach, we proceeded to Bravo's cabin for the purpose of discovering the best paths across the Island, and rec^d. but little encouragement in reply to our manifold questions. Nothing daunted, however, we started, and in crossing the cultivated tract in the rear of the cabin, stopped to observe two wild goats that had been caught, with but slight injury, by the dogs kept for that purpose. They were lightly formed and looked the personification, or rather the ideal, of agility. The only sure method of catching them is with a gun, as they generally escape to heights inaccessible to man or dog. Not so with the wild hog. These are overtaken by the dogs, but in the sanguinary contests that ensue many of them are killed in the course of a season.

Passing through a cane-brake and 'round the base of a hill, we entered the dense foliage of tropical trees and plants, and commenced our tortuous way along the bed of a small stream, often diverging to avoid a small cascade, or where the deep mire made the stream impassable. We had not advanced more than a quarter of a mile (speaking from facts, not impressions), before the path diverged to the hill's side, occasionally crossing the brook. Over shrub and stone, prostrate tree and tangling vine, through [an] almost impenetrable mass of dark green foliage, now catching at this limb, then holding on by that tree. Thus we proceeded for upwards of two hours, at one time losing our way, and again discovering the track by the blazed trees on either hand; now ascending the side of a hill, more by the use of the hands than the feet, clinging to the long tendrils and vines, or pliant roots of the trees, which, protruding from out the bank, hung like so many ropes, to our great convenience.

At last we reached the summit of a hill, and above the murmur of the rustling leaves came the pleasant sound of distant breakers singing

Webb has gone in the Am Whale Ship Bowditch as 1st Mate
but will return again, Collins has been twenty two Years on
the Island, and is an old quiet Man! Bravo is a Young
Man, born on the Island - his father English, his Mother a
Woman. His father is now in California and owner of
two or three Ships. Besides these there are about a dozen Sailors, who
May or May not remain on the Island and a few   men.
Sweet Potatoes, Onions, Sugar Cane, turtle, hogs, goats and bananas
are all they produce at present upon the Island, but by Next
year they will have Several other varieties of Vegetables, the Seeds
given them by Commodore Perry, who at the Same time placed
a number of Sheep and Cattle upon adjoining Islands, the
former are increasing fast, some being Cape Sheep, but one if
the bulls is dead, they hear the bellow of the Cows, but have
never Seen them as yet.

7 Port Lloyd, Peel Island

on the beach. Without delay we descended, irregardless [sic] of the path, and, emerging from out the woods, found ourselves standing upon the broad white sand beach of Pleasant Bay.[71] Breaking off a leaf from a bush near at hand, turned it into the cornucopia and refreshed ourselves with a cool draught from a clear brook at our feet. Then seating ourselves upon a canoe drawn up upon the beach, we indulged in the luxury of a cheroot.

Being rested, we [took] off our shoes and stockings and commenced strolling along the beach, searching for red coral and shells. My friend soon tired of this and ascended the steep declivities above to enjoy the fine prospect around, whilst I lingered among the caverns of the rocks, listerning, almost in awe, to the deep sounding billows, as they rolled in upon them and threw their showers of spray around me. Presently I spied the pointed back fins of several sharks cutting their way through the waves in search of prey; there a shoal of porpoises gamboled by, and were in their turn replaced by the torpid movements of the ponderous turtle, who with upreared head drew in a deep draught of breath, and then disappeared beneath the surface. Still the shark fin appeared in view and cut waters with noiseless motion. They abound in great numbers around these islands and approach within a few feet of the shore.

A distant cheer called my attention and looking up I descried my friend standing on a declivity about four hundred feet above me. I answered with a shout. He pointed seaward, and I distinguished the word, 'Sharks!'

In what dread are these fish held by seamen! With what pleasure do they sacrifice a large piece of pork, when it is intended to cover the iron hook which is suspended astern for their especial benefit! How cheerily they walk him aboard when caught, the suckers hanging to his sides, like fast friends; the little pilot fish then swimming about as if their occupation were gone, but woe to them if he escapes the hook, for piloting him to danger! Landed on the deck, how fierce his struggles, how strong his death throes, implacable to the last. Conquered in body but not in spirit, he dies unresigned to his ignominious fate—a sea pie!

Climbing up the steep hill's side by the pendant roots of the trees, toiling through almost impenetrable masses of brushwood and dense foliage, we at last found ourselves at an elevation above all vegetation

---

[71] Susaki-kō.

except a thick growth of rank grass, breast high. Wading through this, facilitated at times by the tracks of wild hogs, we at last reached the summit of the hills, covered with coarse herbage interspersed with stunted fir and [*crumeno*] bushes,[72] the latter covered with their fragrant white flowers, contrasting pleasantly with the bluebells and yellow buttercups which abounded in sheltered nooks.

But our attention was particularly called to the widespread and picturesque panorama which lay at our feet, amply repaying for [sic] any attending exertions in gaining this elevated position. At our feet lay Pleasant Bay, the roar of the breakers lost in the distance. Opposite, rose Goat Island;[73] and between rolled the restless waves of the ocean, whilst on the left we discerned two or three small reef-bound islands, off one of which the *Plymouth's* missing boat was last seen.

Now turn inward. With a graceful sweep the hills descend to the valleys beneath, and the thick green foliage there luxuriating looks from above like a carpet of verdure spread out by the hands of Nature. Another range of undulating hills, less lofty than ours—beyond, the sea, and on its bosom rides our noble ship, now to all appearances no larger than a pleasure boat, whilst near her rise from the water's edge lofty peaks, perhaps fifteen hundred feet high, their sharp angular edges clearly defined in contrast with the deep blue of the sky. Still further on, thirty or forty miles beyond these, stretches the vast expanse of the ocean till sea and sky blend in one. The power of vision here ceases, and that of thought begins, carrying the attentive gazer in his mental sight to scenes as fair to him in other lands.

Retracing our steps, we reached the ship late in the afternoon, and sat down with invigorated appetite to turtle steaks and the various *et cetera* of an island dinner. As a contrast, let me state [that] some of my shipmates had passed the day sitting in boats dragging for a lost anchor,[74] and thus it is that recreation for a time is purchased by those who follow the sea.

The sudden strong blast that came down from the down [sic] highlands renders this harbour dangerous for boat sailing, and, striking the ship, tautened the cables with a jerk. It was by this means that one of

---

[72] A native term. I am unable to identify the plant.

[73] Yagi-jima.

[74] From the Report of Captain Abbot to Commodore Perry, May 2, 1854: '. . . .I regret to have to report the loss of a bower anchor and thirty fathoms of chain-cable at Port Lloyd, by the parting of the chain or its getting unshackled. . . . In consequence of this mishap, it cost all hands two days' incessant labor in efforts to recover it, and I lament to say without success.' THE EXPEDITION OF AN AMERICAN SQUADRON. v. 2, p. 129.

8 *Pleasant Bay with Goat Island in Distance*

our cables came unshackled, and we have lost our best bower and fifteen fathoms of chain.

Seining is a pleasant amusement and a profitable source of pleasure to those who have for any length of time been reduced to salt-mahogany, old horse—alias, salt beef. With what care is it [the seine] laid in its circular sweep, how knowingly the corks bob up and down on the surface of the water as if participating in the expected fun. And when in the course of time the drag-ropes are man[ned], with what a pull and haul all together the anxious fishermen draw upon the beach the treacherous meshes which have ensnared the unwary inhabitants of the deep; and how they struggle to escape, and at last lie panting upon the shore, their shining scales still glistening with the salt spray of their native element!

Bucket after bucket is filled and sent to the ship and the pleasant sound of something frying (you know what) salutes the ear as you [are] coming on board, somewhat fatigued and considerably wet, but, above all, very sharp set. With just sufficient delay to admit of your brushing up a bit, you take your seat at the table, and are greeted with the pleasant odor of fried mullet. Such have been to me some of the pleasures of today, the very remembrance of which suggests the idea of rehearsal of the same piece.

APRIL 27TH

THIS morning I landed on the beach to put up the target afresh which had been blown down druing the night. The sandy soil affording but imperfect means of support to the poles on which the target was stretched, I looked round and discovered a tree near-by, the trunk of which, about eight feet from the ground, extended in a horizontal direction. Directing some of the boat's crew to climb up with the axes and lop off the branches, I fastened the ploes with spun yarn securely to it, stretched the canvas upon them, and laced it up and down on either side. It has resisted securely a fresh blow during the day, and tomorrow we will have target practice.

The day being fine, though windy, I determined to exercise the launch's crew with their howitzer, not having had before during the cruise an opportunity to do so.

Reaching the boat, we got out the skids, shifted the howitzer from the boat to the field carriage, and landed it. I then gave them their stations in artillery exercise, and went through the several move-

ments of the drill. It is a very difficult thing to make seamen comprehend the necessity of everything being executed according to a regular
routine, and we here meet with much more difficulty than is experienced in the Army where the opportunities of discipline are so much
greater, they being able to resort to many modes of punishment—
highly efficacious—which if carried out on board the ship would prove
of very great inconvenience in rough weather where the services of
all the crew are required.

Fearing to fire among the hills—not knowing but someone might
be walking in that direction—I chose a long sand-beach, and, station-
ing the piece at one end, we fired two rounds at a dead tree; but the
shells exploding against a high rock immediately behind, the pieces
flew back over our heads and fell in the sand behind us, which caused
me to cease firing and shift my ground. My next position was upon a
level piece of ground. Pointing the howitzer out towards the harbour,
I sighted it myself at a rock about a third of a mile off, and the shell
struck it fair. Tried several more rounds, and then returned to the
ship.

This evening they gave up the anchor as lost, having parted a haw-
ser and lost the chain-slings of one of our yards in endeavouring to
weigh coral rocks, supposing them to be the anchor.

APRIL 28TH

BEING my morning watch, and expecting to pay anchor in the afternoon, I left the ship at six in charge of the Osceola [Otaheitan][75] having volunteered to do so that I might see something more of the
island. Our destination lay to a bay to the southward of the one in
which we were anchored, but to reach which required a pull of three
miles. This we attempted to shorten by pulling across a shoal, but
found there was not sufficient water. If it had not been for the sharks
which we could see swimming round us, we might have got out and
shoved the boat over, which, of course, under the circumstances, we
did not do.

So nothing remained but to pull round the headland, a precipitous,
rocky cliff about four hundred feet in height and presenting a perpendicular surface of two or three hundred yards in width. Passed a
canoe turtling, and pulled close in to the base of the cliff so that our

---

[75] This copper-colored Otaheitan who hardly spoke any English, guided a few mem-bers of the *Susquehanna* through the island in 1853.

9 *Pilot's Residence*

oars nearly touched the rocks. It was [an] imposing sight to look up at the immense boulders of rocks suspended over our heads, jutting out into the air and appearing about to loose their hold and fall into the waves beneath them.

Passing through a narrow channel with rocks and breakers on either hand, we opened the adjoining bay, the opposite side of which was formed by the most southerly point of the Island, which consisted of large detached rocks of various shapes, one being very much like a house, and designated in consequence 'Aunt Peggy's House'. Entering an arm of the bay, we passed a remarkable rock, the base of which had been worn through by the action of the waves, leaving a hole about ten feet by six, through which the swell rolled with great force.

Near here we landed at the residence of a man named Antonio, of whom I procured nine barrels of sweet potatoes and then pulled for the residence of the pilot, which I found to be situated at the head of the bay. His house was very comfortable and his outhouse strong and substantial. In one end hung his hammock. Over a table was suspended a collection [of] books, and near-by were a gun, a brace of pistols, two or three hatchets, and a few farming tools.

Directing the men to get the turtles into the boat, I sat down in the cabin, and, handing a cheroot to the pilot, smoked one myself. Then adjourned to the kitchen, situated in a log house near-by, and I there drank with great satisfaction a large tin pot of tea.

From here we went to the turtle-house, hauled a number of big fellows out, turned them on their backs and dragged them down to the boat, where, seated on a canoe sucking sugar-cane, I superintended their embarkation, not an easy operation by any means. Sometimes a big fellow would commence flirt[ing] his fins, throwing the water and sand round him in blinding quantities, much to the diversion of those not within his reach; and as I was the only one so situated, I had all the fun to myself.

The pilot with one of his assistants, a young Frenchman, started in his canoe for the ship, intending to pass through the narrow channel, which would admit of his canoe but not my boat, leaving his cabin in charge of his man Friday, who in this case was a lame Kanaka, he having been bitten a few days previous by a turtle.

Shortly after, I started myself, with a deeply ladened boat, having fifteen turles, weighing on an average about 350 pounds each, besides the potatoes. Returned to the ship as I came, solacing myself during the long pull by sucking sugar-cane and looking at the scenery. Occasionally we tried to hook one of the many turtles that appeared in sight, but did not succeed on account of the noise our oars made.

As we neared the ship, they commenced firing at the target, and I noticed that the second shot passed right through the centre of the canvas, Fired three rounds from each gun, six passing through the target; and all would have struck a ship in the same situation. The distance was about two-thirds of a mile, and the woods in the rear of the target showed the wide furrows and deep gaps of the shell as they had passed on their flight of destruction.

At 10 a.m., whilst heaving up our anchor, an American whaler hove in sight off the harbour. She proved to be the [Bayard][76] belonging to [Wells & Carpenter], six months out from the United States, with 200 barrels of sperm, bound to the Yellow Sea, [Sandwich Islands] having been her last stopping place. Hove to outside for one of boats.

Accompanied by the Doctor[77] I boarded the whaler and purchased 250 gallons of sperm. Found his first officer in a dying state, [and] the Doctor advised his remaining on the Island, [since] fresh air would be beneficial. He said he would remain 'and have a grave upon the land,' remarked the Doctor, finishing the sentence after we left the ship. Our boat returning, filled away at 7 p.m. and set studding sails.

The following day was clear and beautiful, wind light from the southeast. The weather continued the same during the night, and first part of the following day, [the] wind gradually freshening and hauling to the southwest. At near meridian made a remarkable rock to windward and hauled up for it. At 1 p.m. were abreast of and eight miles from it. We judged it to be about three or four hundred feet in height, and from its peculiar form we named it 'Neptune's Finger.'[78] This rock was seen by [Horsburgh][79] in 1802, but, his chronometers

---

[76] The *Bayard* from Greenport, New York, under one Captain Graham, sailed on August 11, 1853. The *Report of Commissioner of Fish and Fisheries* does not give the date of her return. Neither the log of the *Macedonian* nor Captain Abbot's letter to Commodore Perry, dated May 2, mentions the first officer who was in a dying state.

[77] Dr. James S. Gilliam, of whose work Captain Abbot writes: '. . . .visited the sick at Port Lloyd—there being a number of sick men left there from whaleships, upon one of whom they [sic] performed a surgical operation, left him in a fair way of recovery; but for the timely aid and assistance, the man could probably never recover.' THE EXPEDITION OF AN AMERICAN SQUADRON. V. 2, p. 130.

[78] Lot's Wife or Azuma-iwa is a tall, pinnacled rock rising to an elevation of about 250 feet above the sea.

[79] James Horsburgh (1762–1836), hydrographer, was born at Elie in Fifshire, England, and went to sea at the age of sixteen. From very early he began collecting information and observations bearing on the navigation of the eastern seas, and the first result of his labours was the construction of three charts. From April 1802 to February 1804 while commanding the *Anna* in the East, he kept a continuous register of the barometer, taken every four hours, and established the diurnal variation of the barometer in the open sea between the latitudes of 26° N. and 26° S.

being inaccurate, he could not lay it down. Since then we find no mention of it. Hove to and sounded, but found no bottom.

Filled away on our course and made St. Peter's Island ahead. We were now going eleven knots and the breeze freshening. Large masses of clouds gathered along the weather horizon with every indication of coming squalls; in consequence of which, handed our light sails. At 5 p.m. passed to windward of St. Peter's Island about two miles. Its summit was hid by a black cloud, which hung like a pall over its top, giving it a dreary appearance. When we sighted it before, its sharp peak rose high through the clear blue air, but far in the distance.

Whilst still abreast of St. Peter's, a heavy gale sprung up and hauled ahead. This obliged us to reef down. During the night experienced blustering weather. The following day it blew heavily and we carried sail hard, but were obliged eventually to take double-reefs again. The next morning (my watch) the wind abated some and hauled fair, thus completing the circuit of the compass since our departure from Bonin.

At 7 [a] m. made Abbott's House—off Mississippi Island.[80] Shortly after, the wind headed us and became light. In the afternoon we found ourselves abreast of our port but eight miles to leeward near Rock Island.[81] We here encountered tide-rips of such strength as to render the ship unmanageable for some time. They at last passed us, and we could mark their course upon the water miles off. One of the *Powhatan's* and also one of the *Vandalia's* boats came off to us; and a few minutes after, a firm breeze springing up, we stood in and anchored at the mouth of the harbour, in consequence of our sailing again in a few days.

We immediately sent off 30 or 40 turtle[s] to the squadron, which will prove, no doubt, on the morrow a pleasing variety to their daily fare. We sent one to Breese[82] and his mess, which called forth a note of warm thanks in return.

As I gazed over the beautiful landscape spread before me this afternoon, I thought that the hills crowned with trees, their sides sloping gracefully to the water's edge and covered with verdure, to be as pretty a sight as I had seen for a long time.

---

[80] To-shima.
[81] Kamiko-jima.

[82] Kidder Randolph Breese (1831–81) of the *Mississippi*.

C

Visit to Simoda, One of the Two Commercial Ports Opened to Trade By the Treaty

MAY 30TH,[83] 1854

SIMODA is a Japanese speaport town situated at the mouth of Yedo Bay, containing, I should think, about twenty thousand inhabitants, perhaps more. The harbour I should judge to be more than a mile in depth by a third in width; depth of water from twenty to five fathoms, holding ground good. The land round is very hilly, with wide and beautiful valleys intervening. The whole face of the country, excepting inaccessible declivities and the summits of the hills which are intentionally [sic] well-wooded, and where are situated many of their temples and sacred groves, presents a pleasing view of vigorous cultivation, with careful husbandry. One or two small islands are situated in the harbour, but the water round them is deep, and in some respects they are very useful, affording a lee to vessels in blowy weather.

Landing this morning in a small but well-sheltered bay, near the mouth of a small stream which courses through the whole length of the town, we proceeded along a well-paved road, with large pine trees flanking it on either hand. We soon came to a neat building, of one story (like all the house). This we knew to be the place where all business or traffic was transacted, for as yet the valuation of our money has not been determined upon; Government officers attend here, of course.

Continuing on, we entered the town, proceeding up one street, then down another, until we had walked through its whole extent, stopping at the stores occasionally to price articles of lacquer or china-ware, few of which were, however, of a good quality. The crapes were superior to these. Not so the silks.

---

[83] This should be April 30th.

Visited also several temples which are so much alike that the description of one will answer for all. They invariably stand some distance back from the street and have a considerable space round filled with tall fir trees and gravestones, the newest of which were generally decorated with floral offerings arranged in stone vases of simple construction. The entrance is through a stone archway, along a well-paved path, along which are ranged trees and sometimes plants. Ascending a flight of stone steps, with rough statuary on either hand representing uncouth human figures,[84] or those of animals—half dog, half lion—you arrive at an open space surrounding the temple, paved with flag-stones. In the centre of this is the place of worship, a building about fifty feet square by forty in height, with a wooden portico extending round, and near-by is erected a small stone three feet by one and a half, and in shape very much resembling a French coffee cup.

Entering the temple, you find yourself in a large room covered with matting. In each corner stands a large gong. Rude paintings adorn the walls, representing often scenes very foreign to the intention of the edifice. One, I remember, was a painting representing a rab[bit] hunt, another delineated a domestic scene something like a family gathering, but still there were others showing in their homely way a storm upon the ocean with rocks behind, and a tempest-tossed junk in front on the verge of shipwreck. Near to such hung a number of short tails after the manner in which the Japanese wear their hair. These had been cut off and hung up as offerings by the grateful survivors, for their preservation from death. In looking at these little objects of a grateful heart, I thought of Columbus, returned from his dangerous voyage, walking bare-footed to the house of prayer to offer up thanks for his safe return, and, though heathens, I involuntarily respected the feelings which had prompted the act.

The altar railing at the opposite end of the room enclosed the roughly carved though highly ornamented figures of Tosh. The altar coverings consisting principally of silver paper flowers and copper vases. In one of the temples and within the altar railing, we discovered two or three artillery carriages, of foreign pattern, though native make.

On inquiry it proved that the building had lately been occupied by troops. Another temple was situated upon the side of a hill conical in shape, the ascent being made by a flight of regular stone steps one

---

[84] They are not human figures, but the *Niwo* or Deva kings, guardians of the temple gate.

Whilst still abreast of St Peters a heavy gale sprung up and hauled ahead, — this obliged us to ref down. During the night experienced blustering matther. The following day it blew heavily and we carried sail hard, but were obliged eventually to take double refs again. The next morning (my watch) the wind abated some and hauled fair, thus completing the cir-

10 *St. Peter's Island*

hundred and eight in number.[85] From here we had a fine view of the town and valley beneath.

Young Adams had been invited by an acquaintance, a mandarin,[86] who had visited the day previous and who had formerly resided in Kanagawa when the squadon were [sic] at anchor off that town, to visit him at this present lodgings, which were temporary only, his permanent residence being in Yedo, and myself accompanied him, a guide leading the way. We were shown into one of the better class of buildings with the Emperor's flag[87] festooned in front, which I afterwards discovered was the distinguishing mark of mandarin's dwelling. We were cordially rec^d. and shown into the back room of the house which opened upon a miniature garden, representing a country house with trees around (they [are] dwarfed to suit the scene). A bridge span[ned] a small stream filled with goldfish.

The mandarin was a young man with a pleasant expression of countenance, neatly dressed, and had been engaged [in] writing prior to our entrance. He handred us a book off his low desk or table, which he had evidently been referring to. It was a military work copied from the Dutch, with excellent plates representing the various pieces of European field artillery and other can[non] comparing it, no doubt, with our own, which he had examined during his visits to the various ships of the squadron.

Seating ourselves, refreshments soon followed, consisting of remarkably fine tea and sweetmeats, the latter put up very nicely in neat wooden boxes with inner coverings of transparent paper, and served in the same. About this time another official[88] joined us (one of those appointed to ap[praise] purchased articles). He spoke a little English and through him princincipally, we carried on the conversation. A number of paper fans being produced, we were reqeusted to write our names upon them, which we did, N.[89] also drawing a ship upon one, and I, a view of the harbour of Peel Island upon another. This pleased them very much.

We then exchanged cards—the name of the mandarin sounded in

---

[85] According to the Buddhist belief, there are one hundred and eight wordly desires which bind man's soul to the life of sin. His salvation comes only when these cravings are stilled and his soul is united with the Whole. Whether he goes up a flight of steps or listens to the bell of one hundred and eight strokes, his prayer is to set his soul free from the limitations of the material world.

[86] A Manchu term erroneously applied to a Japanese official.

[87] The flag of the Shōgun, and in this case, the house belonged to a *hatamoto* or banner knight, who was the unfiefed *samurai* in the service of the Shogunate.

[88] This probably was Shintarō Nakadai, petty officer of the *Kanjō-bugyō*, finance bureau of the Shogunate.

[89] N. B. Adams.

English being Gohads Esafudor.[90] One of the company present was a doctor who spoke Dutch and read and wrote English a little. He wrote his name in English as Doctor Kuoket.[91] *Sake* was then handed round, the remainder of the sweet meats rolled up in paper and handed to us (according to Japanese custom). We then took our departure, they politely presenting us, unasked, with umbrellas, it having commenced to rain.

In the afternoon we walked round to a bathing establishment and stood for some time looking on at the scene, much to the astonishment of the little ones, who, with the hot water streaming down their faces, still managed to keep one eye upon us in open amazement. I made two or three small purchases, but as there is to be a general exhibition of articles for sale on our return about the middle of June, I determined to wait until that time, as offering better opportunities than the present.

Returned to the ship at sundown in a drenching rain. During the night, it blew great guns from the northeast, but as we tailed out shore, we only gave her a good scope of chain and rode it out without dragging. Since our arrival until today, May 5, we have had a long swell on, causing the ship to roll as if we were at sea.

MAY 6TH

This morning we [pulled] up anchor and stood out of the harbour. The *Vandalia* and *Southampton* did the same, being under the land at first, and, the wind dying away, the *Vandalia* ranged ahead of us; but suddenly the wind hauled and came out fresh. Bracing up, we shot past the *Vandalia*, and went about. Commenced beating through the passage between Ohosima and Volcano Islands.[92] At meridian weathered the latter, and stood to the northward heading up clear of the former, the *Vandalia* ten miles to leeward and the *Southampton* about twelve.

At 4 p.m. passed Ohosima [and] noticed two little fishing towns[93] at its base, whilst from its summit rose a small spiral column of smoke. My sketch in the beginning of this book represents this smoky column, an underfined mass impelled down its side by the force of the northeast

---

[90] Esaburō Gohara acted as a mentor to Einosuke Moriyama, interpreter to the Commissioners. Little is known about him.

[91] Dr. Ryōan Kurokawa (1817–90). As a boy he studied Dutch and medicine in Nagasaki, and was a physician to the Kanazawa clan.

As a liberal leader, he advocated Japan's intercourse with Western nations.

[92] I do not think Sproston meant the Volcano Islands or Kazan Retto, which are south of the Bonins, but rather the volcanic islands of Idzu.

[93] Villages Motomura and Habuminato.

the passage between Ohosima and volcano Islands. At
Meridian weathered the latter, and stood to the Northward
heading up clear of the former. The Vandalia ten miles to
leward and the Smithampton about twelve

The above is a rough outline of our position at Meridian.

22

11 *Seven Islands of Izu*

gale blowing at the time. Then snow lined its top and sides. Now all is bright and green, forming a pleasant contrast.

Clear, beautiful, moonlight night. Not a cloud in the sky. Ship going 12 and 13 knots and hour, wind fresh, and sea smooth. This cannot last—the Japan Sea is unused to such weather. In the mid-watch the clouds begin to gather, the wind freshens and hauls a head, and Sunday morning[94] opens upon us with a strong reef topsail breeze and a cross sea. Sunday afternoon the wind became light. This day found ourselves one hundred miles from land, and not much to the northward in consequence of our not having hugged the shore more when the wind was fair. The following day proved nearly calm, but that night it came out fair and fresh; and with steering sails set both sides, we run [sic] off about 150 miles.

The barometer falling rapidly towards morning led us to expect bad weather, but instead of a gale a thick dense fog enveloped us, so heavy and impenetrable that we could not see a half a ship's length off. Having neared the land during our night's run, we considered it unsafe to carry sail in this situation on an unknown coast, so that reducing our speed to four or five knots we continued on our course during the day, the breeze gradually growing lighter until it at last died away, leaving us still wrapped in our murky shroud.

This in time passed away, and the next wind that sprang up was ahead. At four in the morning when I came on deck, I found the ship by the wind under close reefs, but in an hour's time, by permission of the Captain, I had her under topgallant sails bowling along with a fine fresh breeze nine or ten knots on a wind. The sun rose clear and the morning was beautiful. The glittering spray sparkled on our decks, forced by the wind over our weather bow. The bracing air made me feel like shouting, but I kept my hands in my pocket, for to us it was bitter cold, it having only been week or so previous since we had the thermometer standing at 70° and 80° when in Lloyed Harbours. Now it was below 40°, showing that heat and cold are always comparative. I myself am opposed to anything under 70°, but this is only a matter of taste.

Got a cast of the lead [but] no bottom.

A few moments after and the cry came from the lookout aloft, 'Land O! Where away? High land right ahead and on the weather bow!'

---

[94] May 7th.

After a while it was reported stretching out to leeward. Reported it to the Captain and put ship about, but in half an hour went about again, and discovered the *Southampton* to leeward standing with us. At nine, having neared the land considerably, we could plainly discern the summits of the high hills covered with snow, and knew by the general formation of the coast that we were at the entrance to the Sangar Straits[95] (or Sugar Straits—why so called I cannot imagine at it must certainly be too cold for the cane to grow in this latitude). The wind being ahead, made but comparatively little progress during the day.

At sunset close to Point [Shiriya], the most northernmost end of Niphon, with Yeso in sight opposite. The *Southampton* [was] close to us, having had a fair wind at one time, equally contrary our own. We could see her not two miles off with yards braced in, standing across our bows; but about this distance off she lost it. To windward was a ship under easy sail which we rightly supposed to be the *Vandalia*. The night proved clear, and the moon shown [sic] brightly on land and sea, and every now and then, as one of the ships would cross the bright track on the waters her sails would glisten in the moon's rays, and then disappear like the phantom ship we read of, off Cape Good Hope.

The morning when I relieved the deck at eight o'clock, we had a fine leading breeze and were standing up the wide and beautiful Straits of Sangar. The ships were in line: *Vandalia* leading, *Southampton* following. On either hand and distant apart some twenty miles, rose the high and snow-clad hills[96] of Niphon, of Yeso, or Matsmai[97] (Yeso being the original name, Matsmai being the name of the person who conquered it).

Rounding a point of high land (refer to drawing), we opened the wide bay or harbour of Hakodadi [sic] and anchored three miles off the town. The authorities visited the ship in the afternoon [and] the Captain handed them a letter from the government officers of Simoda, stating the reason of our visiting the port; but we do not land until the Commodore arrives with the steamers.

---

[95] Tsugaru Straits, named after the Tsugaru feudal clan that ruled this part of the country since the 12th century.

[96] Komagadake.

[97] Yezo, officially called Hokkaidō, is the northermost of the larger islands that form the Japanese archipelago. In the early 17th century, the Shōgun Ieyasu Tokugawa granted the island to one Yoshihiro Matsumae, who conquered the southwestern part and established his capital at Matsumae, some sixty miles to the southwest of the present city of Hakodate.

12   *Harbor of Hakodate*

This chart represents the tracks of the three vessels.[98] The *Vandalia* and *Southampton*, hugging the land, discovered that it extended out too much to the e[astwar]d on the chart, whilst our ship, standing out to sea, found a strong E.N.E. current and irregular sea. Winds variable in both cases and of short duration from any one quarter.

---

[98] The chart is missing in the manuscript.

Description
of
Hakodade

MAY, 1854

THE town of Hakodade is situated at the base of a lofty prom[ontory] which extends out into the straits of Sangar for upwards of two miles, and is connected with the Island of Yeso or Matsmai by a narrow, level strip of land covered with hillocks of sand. The highest point of the prom[ontory] is directly over the middle of the town, and is, I should say, full a tousand feet in height. Upon this elevated situation a lookout is situated which commands an extended view for miles round, and, I might add, nearly the whole lenght of the Straits.

The sides of the hills to within about three hundred feet of the base are void of all vegetation (except a covering of thick dark-green grass, which had a very pleasing effect when viewed from the harbour). At this height there is a grove of fir trees, with tall stems and spreading tops, sweeping round the side of the hill with a graceful curve. About the same height and near to the fir grove, is a temple with a broad [paved] path leading up to it from the town beneath. There are also several winding paths leading to the summits above, which in consequence admit of easy access. The side of the prom[ontory] opposite to the town is much more precipitous, and its shores reef-bound and but thinly inhabited.

Having now given a general idea of the appearance of the prom [ontory], I will proceed to describe the harbour and anchorage, which are of considerable beauty, both in form and convenience.

Hakodade and its harbour (it has been remarked by many officers) bears a strong resemblance to Gibralter being on a scale of one-third in respect to comparative size with the former. [Both have] the same high, bold prom[ontory]; the towns erected at their bases, connected in both cases by a level strip of land with the main country; their signal hills alike; the wide-sweeping curvature of the heads of the bays; the broad, level sand beaches on the opposite shores, and the little villages there situated, connecting with the towns by roads along sea side; the high precipitous hills on the opposite side, resembling Ape's Hill on the coast of Africa. There is also Europa Point with its batteries (in this case, however, only a small fort), with the exception of the Lion's Head, and that the highlands, even as late as the beginning of summer are tipped with snow, the resemblance is striking to one familiar with the appearance of the two places. In both cases the small-class sailing crafts anchor near the shore and the head of the bay, whilst the larger vessels lie a mile or two off from the town.

I will now endeavor to give a description of this Japanese town, and from my observation so far I am led to suppose that in most respects they all bear a strong resemblance to each other in mode of building, habits, customs, and internal laws, as well as in dress and manners, change of climate making but little difference.

Hakodade as I have before mentioned, is built at the base of the prom[ontory]. It extends along the level land and half the circuit of the head of the bay, but is very thinly inhabited in that quarter, I should say it contained about thirty five thousand inhabitants, few of whom are in affluent circumstances. There is one principal or business street running the whole length of the town and near the water, from which it is only separated by a row of *wams* (sic) and houses. In this street are all the stores, custom-house, government buildings, and *et cetera* [sic]. With the exception of two or three above, all the other streets tend at right angles with this one, and terminate in it.

I will now proceed to describe my first visit ashore.

The morning, fortunately, was clear and pleasant. I say fortunately because it had been blowing fresh from every point of the compass since our arrival, accompanied by rain, and the air consequently moist and chilly. We accidentally landed at the Government Council House (afterwards set apart as the Commodore's quarters), and at that time the flag lieutenant was holding an audience and making preparations for a meeting or visit of explanation between the Governor[99] and Commodore on the following day.

We walked through the court at the rear of the building on mats placed there for the purpose, and, attended by a two-sworded official, proceeded along the main street, which was lined on each side with curious spectators in a stooping position (as a mark of respect). This

[99] Takahiro Matsumae, lord of the Fukuyama Castle.

the Commodore very properly forbid [sic] when he became cognizant of the fact.

I noticed that the houses on each side were closed with but few exceptions, although they offered no objection to my entering when I wished to light a cigar. Passed down the whole length of the street, which, like the rest of the town, was divided off by gates into wards; and as we passed from one ward to another, we changed officers, they never proceeding out of their own ward. The street at the lower end terminated at a moderate-sized temple. The interior, however, was quite roomy and well fitted up.

Retracing our steps, we proceeded in the opposite direction. Passing the custom-house, continuing on for two or three squares, we turned to the right and soon entered the spacious court in front of the Great Temple,[100] larger than any I have seen in Japan or China. In the middle of the open space stood a handsome fir tree, brought when small from Russia. On the right were a long row [of] comfortable buildings in which the priests resided, and directly in front stood the Temple, with a wide portico in front, and massive stone steps. On the left rose the belfry.

I will first give an exterior view of this, the finest building I have seen in the country, and then describe the interior.

The interior of this temple is both lofty and spacious, of a square form, and on all sides, about six feet from the walls, the flooring is raised a foot higher, the whole covered with white mats, the edges of which are bound with blue. At intervals on twelve feet apart and round this platform extend rows of highly polished wooden pillars with cornices of the same material, which is of a dark walnut colour. A balustrade extends along the front, an open, space being left, by which to enter.

At the opposite end is the altar railing, and beyond, the altar, which for its simplicity and beauty deserves a somewhat minute description. Formed of wood, highly polished and finely gilded; ornamented by a shrine with a small figure in front, robed in flowing garments and a halo round its head. On each side of the shrine stand metal vases filled with artificial flowers and leaves of a large size, silver-gilded. The whole presents a pleasing effect, and a much superior finish to anything I had expected to find in this country. On each side, but further back, stood smaller altars with only vases upon them. The ascent to

---

[100] Jōgenji Temple of the Shingon sect.

the altar is by three broad steps, and the floor composed of dark broad boards, smooth and glossy. Immediately over the altar railing is a remarkably fine piece of carving in wood representing flowers, vines, serpents, cranes, and other allegorical figures, symbolical of their religion. A large metal lamp hung in the open space, paper being substituted for glass (such is the case throughout the country). Priests both young and old with shaven heads and robed in long gowns, accompanied us in our examination. They possessed but little dignity or gravity of manner. The whole scene reminded me forcibly of a Catholic church, and I doubt not the same has been the impression of many.

Leaving the Temple we continued up the main street, the officers accompanying us, obliging the people to shut their houses as we passed; this [we] endeavoured to prevent by holding them back whenever they attempted to precede us. This they remedied, however, by motioning to the officers at the different stations, who appeared readily to understand them. We at last reached a gate that was closed. They here made signs for us to return, which, of course, we disregarded; opening it, passed through.

We now passed the portion of the town off which the junks were anchored, and had proceeded a short distance round the head of the bay. The houses here were of the poorer kind and scattered. Outside of the gate we encountered a party of Japanese soldiers gambling with their copper money; opposite to them stood a small fort or stone enclosure, but without guns.

Retracing our steps, on our way back stopped in at a barber's shop. I was much amused to notice the similarity of objects which greeted my view on entering. In front sat a Japanese undergoing the process of shaving; only, in this case, part of the head as well as the face was covered with soap. Behind him was another having his hair dressed, differing again in this respect, that the queue was formed on top of the head in place of being suspended behind. From the walls hung notices of theatrical and wrestling performances with appropriate illustrations, showing that they have amusements in the town in which we cannot participate from our want of knowledge of localities (as they would not direct us).

We next entered a graveyard, in which was a garden of flowers. I am led to suppose from the proximity of the rude stone figures which mark the resting place of the dead, that they must be interred in an upright position; but little care apparently had been taken of the

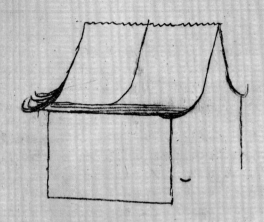

The interior of this temple is both lofty and spacious, of a square form, and on all sides about six feet from the walls, the flooring is raised a foot higher, the whole covered with white mats, the edge of which are bound with blue. At intervals of twelve feet apart and round this flat form extends rows of highly polished wooden pil with cornices of the same material, which is of a dark walnut colour. A balustrade extends along the front, an open space being left, by which to enter. At the opposite end is the Alter railing, and beyond the alter, which from its simplicity and beauty deserves a somewhat minute description Formed of wood, highly polished and finely gilded, an Shrine with a small bronze figure in front, robed in flowing garments and a hallow round its head, On each side of the shrine stand metal vases filled with artificial flowers and leaves of a large size silver gilded the whole presents a pleasing effect, and a much superior finish to any thing I had expected to find in this country. On each side but further back stood smaller alters with only vases upon them. The ascent to the Alter is by three broad steps, and the floor composed of dark broad boards, smooth and glassy. Immediately over the Alter ceiling is a remarkably fine piece of carving in wood representing flowers, vines, Serpents, Cranes and other allegorical figures Symbolical of their religeon. A large metal lamp hung in the open space, paper being substituted for glass (such is the case through out the Country). Priests both young and old with shaven heads, and robed in long gowns accompanied us in our examination, they possessed but little dignity or grace gravity of Manner. The whole scene reminded me forcibly of a Catholic curch, and I doubt not the same has been the

graves although many of them, those of most recent construction, were ornamented with chalices of flowers. Here also we saw a rude stone statue in a sitting posture, of a female with two young children in her arms.

The custom-house next attracted our attention. This building is, of course, of substantial construction. The rear or side towards the water is open, displaying the interior of the house, which in that portion is divided into three rooms of moderate size. In the middle [is] one in which the custom-house officers sit all day, receiving reports and transacting business. From the respect shown them they are evidently persons of the first consequence. The custom-house landing is well constructed of stone, but good[s] appear never to be landed there from the junks, from which I judge, and no doubt rightly, they desire no revenue from home trade.

It was in this building that the bazaar for the officers was afterwards held—but of that in due time. In the course of my morning walk I visited several stores, from curiosity and also with the desire of procuring a few articles as samples of their manufactures. In describing one store I describe all, they being very much alike in appearance, and the articles for sale nearly of the same kind and quality. We could generally distinguish a store from a dwelling-house, from the quarter of the town in which it was in and from the fact of samples, such as cotton cloths, corn brooms, and the like, being suspended from the doors.

The interior presents a heterogeneous collection of Japanese household utensils, ornamental and useful, and the material, silk or cotton, of which their apparel is made. The salesman invariably would be found sitting cross-legged on the raised and mat-covered floor which covers nearly the whole of the shop, leaving only a narrow earthen pathway on which his customers stand. From this position he never rises, shop-boys getting down and bringing to him the article inquired for. Before him is placed a wooden box containing a pot with fire in it to light his pipe by, and often tea tray and cup besides, both being in constant use during the day.

The most valuable and bulky articles, such as cotton and silk in the natural or manufactured form, oil paper for rain cloaks, Japanese fancy goods and groceries, are contained in moderate-sized boxes piled one upon the other in regular tiers and opening at the side. Under these and on each side are ranges of small drawers containing tobacco and pipes, tea, perfumery, musk, paper, books, pictures,

India ink, silk and leather pouches for bills or tabacco, and various other articles, some of which I never could understand for what use they were constructed. Besides these and exposed on shelves, are cups, vases, jars, teapots, and the several varieties of porcelain ware, most of them of an inferior quality. In the back part of the shop, the superior kind being boxed up, are kept the different varieties of lacquer-ware. This completes the general assortment of a Japanese store, which from its miscellaneous collection might be likened to a country store at home.

It must really be a natural quality of the American character—something innate—to strike a trade, and I was not behind myself by any means; in fact, I was one of the pioneer assayers, and we managed in this wise: Entering a store, the purchaser would look round for the desired article, or, generally speaking, for anything peculiar to the country, and finding something to suit him would take it down, and placing it before the shop-man, search for something more, until seeing nothing more to suit his fancy, he would then begin to determine the price of each one separately. To a dollar there are 4800 cash or copper coins strung, consequently 2400 to a half-dollar, 1200 to a quarter, and so on down the scale.

Now by establishing the basis that one finger signifies a hundred cash, and that two fingers crossed means fifty cash, you can easily comprehend the manner in which trade was carried on. The officer having completed his pile, holds up one article at a time. This piece of pantomime is answered by a show of fingers on the part of the Japanese, which the officer notes down in his memorandum book. Each in its turn having been thus disposed of, he casts up the total, compares fingers with the shop-man and pays the amount. What could be more simple and to the point? Not the mode home, certainly.

My second visit ashore was confined more par[ticularly] to an observation of the back part of the town, and during our whole tour we were closely followed and somewhat impeded by three Japanese officers, who threw many little obstructions in the way of our movements. However, by establishing it as a general rule of action to go the opposite way to the one directed, managed to get at least an exterior view of all that was to be seen. We found many of the streets in the rear to be inhabited only by the poorer classes, whilst others again were filled with the houses of the rich.

But even these were rather indifferent dwellings, excepting the Governor's dwelling, which formed a hollow square, with pleasure-grounds and a grove of trees around two sides. The entrance, by two large solid doors, reached from the top to the bottom of the house, and near-by were the quarters of the government guard. The Governor whom [we] afterwards saw, was a spare, tall man, rather ungainly in motion, but great dignity of manner, and a decidedly intellectual face and head. How lonely must his life be, midst all his power, his wife and family hostages at Yedo,[101] whilst he holds his present position! (If we trust to the reports of books, this is an invariable Japanese custom.)

Some of the better class of dwellings had stone-walls and hedges in front with gardens of fruit trees and flowers which gave them a much more cheerful appearance. Near one situated on the outskirts of the town, there was a large fir tree, whose branches had been so arranged as to cover a circular space of fully fifty feet, none reaching higher than ten feet from the ground.

Ascending part of the way up the hill by a broad road, we had a fine view of the harbour and town beneath us, the stone-covered roofs at our feet presenting a motly appearance at our feet [sic]. The better class of houses are securely tiled, but the others are roofed with a collection of tiles and thatch kept in position by regular tiers of stones. We often laughingly remarked that such a method would not answer in a country where mobs and fire companies often prevail in numbers and come forth to battle with bricks and other handy missiles.

In the meantime the spirit of trade had been busy, the desire of Japanese curiosities great, the effect upon the stores visible, many having sold out their stock on hand of such articles. Still, opinion was generally entertained, and I full[y] assured in my own mind of the truth of the statements to this day, that the finer vases had been concealed from our sight by the commands of the authorities[102] and the prices raised by such as were displayed. This produced considerable dissatisfaction, and the consequence was, a bazaar was opened under the superintendence of the flag lieutenant[103] and interpreter,[104] the latter properly a missionary in China and a remarkably disagreeable man.

One of the three public rooms of the custom-house was appropriated

---

[101] A system of hostages known as *sankin kōtai*, under which each important feudal lord was compelled to spend several months every year at Yedo, and to leave his wife and family behind when he returned to his fief.

[102] The reason there was no superior ware on this island was that there was no demand, the inhabitants being mostly peasants and fishermen.

[103] Silas Bent (1820–87), oceanographer. His excellent hydrographic surveys in Japanese waters were published by the government in 1857.

[104] Samuel Wells Williams.

D

to the display of goods for sale. I was fortunate enough to be present at the first exhibition, which, however, did not meet my expectations. A few pieces of crape and silk and about a third of the lacquer-ware were worth purchasing, and I may here add that for the several successive days that the bazaar was open, the same might be said of the assortment each day. Want of confidence, as well as the unusually great demand, no doubt acted against us. Time will in all probability overcome both these difficulties, and when once fairly embarked in trade, they will display capabilities in barter and exchange unsurpassed by any other people. Caution with them must be a proverb.

The Commodore had an assortment of goods placed at his disposal of a much finer quality than any I had seen in the stores or at the bazaar, and some of our officers entering unexpectedly the back room of a store, would there find varieties of lacquer-ware, gilded and plain, vastly superior to those exposed to view in the front shops. All this, of course, is somewhat unaccountable, the only reasons that I can advance being those mentioned above, for such an apparent want of reciprocal faith and mutual good understanding on their part. Time only will overcome the prejudice, if I may so call it, engendered by years, even centuries, of non-intercourse with foreign nations. For the Dutch trade hardly deserves the name of commerce, limited, as it is, by so many restrictions.

It is now approaching the last of May, and the hills and valleys round us, which on our first arrival presented but a barren and cheerless aspect to the view, have now cast off in a great measure their winter mantle and robed themselves in the verdure of spring, the winds have become milder, and the sun's rays warmer. The frequent clumps of pines and firs afford a grateful shade after a noon-day's walk along the hot sand beach of the surf-bound coast of the weather-shore, or over the level plains at the foot of the lofty hills whose summits alone still capped with snow tell of cold winter past. But as the shades of evening approach and gather round us, the winds once more resume their force, and the chill night feels like winter's sway. The time of our departure is drawing near, the *Southampton* has already sailed for Simoda, visiting Volcano Bay[105] on her passage. This bay is situated to the northward of Sangar Straits in the Islands of Matsmai, and is only separated from it by a tongue of land which extends out into the sea.

---

[105] Uchiura-wan.

JUNE 1ST

THIS morning the *Vandalia* and our ship got under way, the former bound to Shanghai, sailing along the opposite side of Nippon, whilst we return to Simoda, diverging from our course on the way to survey the waters round the Island of [Hachijō], the penal settlement of the Japanese Empire, situated about a hundred miles to the southward of Simoda. And now the high peninsular bluff of Hakodate is shut out from our view by a dense fog, which, rolling down upon us, wraps us in its murky shroud. The wind which had been light, though fair, has died away, and we drift helplessly at the mercy of the current.

The evening approaches and yet no change, but whilst I write, the ship heels to the breeze, and I am told a strong wind is coming up, but unfortunately ahead. And now we move swiftly through the water, every sail distended to the gale, but whither we can hardly say, as the thick, heavy mist still enshrouds us, so thick that we can scarcely distinguish objects on the deck forward.

Thus for several days have we been sailing on. At one moment the sun shines brightly, the distant land rises clearly in the blue sky, and with the glass you gaze with pleasure upon the alternate scenery of green valley and rugged hill; but suddenly a low dark mass comers rolling down from windward, object after object disappears from the view, until at last the driving mist closes round you, your ship appears to part the murky wall as she clears the waters, and you sail on, as it were, on a strange and unknown sea.

JUNE 4TH

WE are now standing close in to the little town of [Kamaishi][106] pleasantly situated at the base of a range of high hills, and its little white houses form an agreeable contrast with the green background which slopes with a gentle curve to the water's edge, there terminating in a low natural wall which extends for miles. At the base of the wall, is a white sand beach. Though it is cloudy over our heads, we can see the sun's rays shining on the hillsides and glistening on the snow which covers their summits. How beautiful the country looks, in colour a light green, the low undulating meadow-ground dotted with clumps

[106] From the description and the log of the *Macedonian*, this identification, I believe, is correct.

of trees, the hillsides covered with the same, the high ridges crowned by the tall firs, each tree trimmed to exact shape—the whole producing a tableau of sea and land!

Coasting along the shore are many junks, some standing out to sea, but never approaching us. Every now and then a black mass rises out of the sea near us, and from it ascends a column of water. Slowly it disappears from view again, to reappear in another direction; and thus gambols about us a school of whales with slow and uncouth motion. The clouds have now begun to disperse, and in the mist appears the setting sun, making the scene still more cheerful; and as it drinks up the moisture from the earth, misty columns unite both land and sky.

'The sun's rattling down his rigging,' remarked the Captain.

'We shall have wind tonight-and here it comes,' he continued, directing my attention to the whitecapped waves to windward, an indubitable evidence of the approaching breeze. 'Take it in the light sails, sir!'

This was soon accomplished, but not too soon; for a few moments after, as the sun disappeared from view, the strong breeze was upon us, careening us over on our side as we dashed on our way.

'Hands reef topsails!' was the word that soon followed, and during the night it blew a half-gale.

JUNE 6TH

THIS day we run [sic] one hundred and fifty miles and made on our course—how much do you think? Eighteen miles, making short tacks in shore whilst daylight lasts, and at night standing off! We have encountered contrary currents and light head-winds, which would freshen up for a time in the evening, and then die away again. Our passage will be a long one, no doubt, and if it were not for the fair at Simoda on the 15th, I would not regret it. However, we must certainly be in by that time.

Warm, pleasant weather, sun[ny] days, and calm moonlight nights are now our portion. Few can properly appreciate such blessings, as we do. For half a year we have been wearing pea-coats, a singular and unparalleled confession for an East India crusier, but such has been the case; and I for one most gladly hail the grateful feeling of a summer wind, to once more lounge on deck *en dishabille* and indulge your taste for literature *ad libitum*, or inhale the fragrant and narcotic aroma of your meerschaum *sans cérémonie*.

All these little luxuries, for such they are to us truly, we now enjoy to their full extent. These are the great resources of sea life, or, as I might leniently term them, the innocent egotisms of the passing hour. These in connection with the various calls of duty and the frequent brushing up, if I may use the expression, of professional knowledge, form the daily routine of an officer's life at sea. In no sphere of life are the internal resources of the individual more called in play, or his mind more tasked to discover a useful and systematic [way] of passing his time, to enable him to overcome apathy and drive off ennui, especially as his feasts are more apt to be those of reason than of gastronomical delicacies.

But one great truth remains yet to be mentioned; which is, that shipboard is one of the few places where a man's natural character and mental qualifications are sure to be known, and consequently where undue pretensions of any kind are invariably unmasked. This hypothesis being granted, it is to be hoped that human nature has its bright as well as dark colors—as it has. If it were not so, then would ignorance truly be bliss. So much for the moralization of a contented philosophy! And here let it rest.

JUNE 8TH

LAST night a fresh fair wind sprung [sic] up which continues to speed us on our course, though as evening approaches it becomes lighter and will, no doubt, die away as the sun goes down. I have spent most of the day on deck enjoying the fine weather and gazing on the varied features of the landscape, the land being close aboard. This morning I was an early riser, perforce, before the break of day. Then the weather was not quite so agreeable. A heavy irregular swell rocked the ship about with uneasy motion as if it were but a shell upon its surface; the wind blew in strong and fitful gusts, which prevented me from setting the lighter sails; and numerous little rivulets trickled down the back of my tarpaulin coat, emanating from the rim of my southwester, which there collected the falling showers and guided them from [my] neck with the accuracy of a water-spout, much to my gratification.

At daylight made land and steered for it, but soon finding ourselves in a bight, we stood out again and shaped a course along the coast, passing numerous Japanese junks from time to time, as if they were at anchor.

At four in the afternoon, abreast of Cape King,[107] near Yedo Bay. The wind is light and sea smooth. Numerous fishing-boats in sight, but all avoid us until they see the American ensign floating at our peak, when a joyful shout declares their recognition of the flag, and those nearest to us get out their oars, and, aided by sail, scull towards us, seize the ropes thrown to them and, making fast, commence throwing sardine-fish in upon decks.

The appearance of buckets let down by lines to them suggests a more expeditious method of disposing of their fin freight, for which we recompense them with ship biscuit, of which they appear to be very fond. With mutual good wishes, unintelligible except by gesture, we separate, and discuss our savory joy on the following morning with sentiments favourable to the late treaty and its practical benefits as here illustrated.

JUNE 9TH

FINDS us on a clear summer's day, sailing slowly through the group of islands near the mouth of Yedo Bay; when a few months back we encountered violent gales of wind, hail, and snow, the invariable accompaniments of a stormy winter coast, which in our case resulted in something approaching shipwreck, but which, haply [we] escaped. Gave a reef a name.

JUNE 10TH

DURING the night experienced a head-wind and sea which retarded our progress considerably. At ten this morning made the Island [Hachijō], on our weather beam distant twenty five miles, the wind being light. The afternoon found us nearly in the same position except that South Island[108] was in sight ahead. During the first watch the ship approached nearer her course and the breeze freshened. At midnight when I relieved the deck, [Hachijō] could be dimly distinguished on our weather bow, but in two hours we were abreast and not more than three miles distant from it. In obedience to orders reduced sail, hove to, and sounded in 120 fathoms. The next morning when I turned out, we were sailing round the Island, in accordance with our instructions.

---

[107] Nojima-zaki.   [108] Aoga-shima.

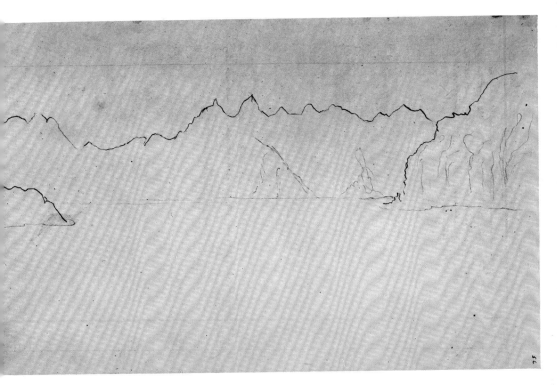

14 *Ko-jima no Seto Channel*

I will now give a description of the Island or Islands, as there proved to be a large and a smaller one.[109] Deriving nearly all my information as to their use from other sources, I will simply remark that these islands are inhabited only by state or other criminals, placed here in expiation of their crimes; besides a few soldiers to keep them in order. The smaller island, which we passed very close to, is separated from the larger by a channel[110] about four miles in width, with a considerable westerly current setting through; of a conical shape, and about one thousand feet in height. Two sides are precipitous and rugged, whilst the others though almost perpendicular, are highly cultivated to the very apex, each patch or gradation of land resembling a step, and on almost every one, two or three houses are erected, built of thatch, with small reservoirs near-by to receive the copious supplies of the frequent showers. Though vegetation was luxuriant, we saw no trees apparently over twenty or thirty feet in height.

Passing to leeward of this, our next track brought us close in to [Hachijō] proper. In shape it was high and conical at each end, and low in the middle. I should say its length was about four miles. On this, the southern side, and about amidships, there was a considerable indentation, forming an open harbour, slightly protected by the smaller island to the southwest. Fishing boats or junks of any kind, of course, they are not allowed; therefore are they entirely dependent upon their own exertions for subsistence. Clothing they procure by the manufacture of silk, they being furnished with the raw material, and it is said to be the finest quality in the Empire.[111] In exchange, they receive coarse cotton cloth for their own use. Such is their weary and isloated life, cut off from all kindred ties and the luxuries of life, in expiation for their crimes.

We spent the day in endeavouring to beat round the Island, but in consequence of light head-winds and strong currents, failed. The night proving rainy and blowy, hove to under topsails. At daylight filled away, made sail, and stood for Broughton's Rock,[112] distant from [Hachijō] thirty miles, and on our course for Simoda. At about eight a.m. passed the Rock and made a number of islands ahead.

[109] Ko-jima.

[110] Ko-jima no Seto.

[111] Hachijō silk is famous for its fine weave as well as brillian color. The natives use *kariyasu* (Arthraxon Ciliare, *Beauv*), *kiwada* (Phellodendron amurense *Rupr.*) as well as clay for dye.

[112] Inanaba-shima.

Return
to
Simoda

JUNE 12TH

THIS day, June 12th, visited Simoda, and found the inhabitants much more trustful in their intercourse, although, negotiations being in progress at the time between the Commodore and seven of the Japanese Council, all trade was forbid [sic] by the Commodore. In company with a friend rambled through the town; found the shops open, and the people engaged at their daily occupations. The larger temples are now occupied by the princes and their retainers, each having a white cotton curtain festooned round both the entrance and the building itself, with the appropriate device of each painted in black upon them, and here soldiers and attendants are continually running about in haste, showing their strict attention to the slightest command of their masters.[113]

The country is in full leaf and flower, and during our absence one harvest has been gathered and another is being planted. Before almost every door are pile[d] shocks of wheat, and the women are busily engaged pounding the heads in their large mortars, to separate the grain—a very tedious method of accomplishing the object, as anyone might readily suppose. The straw is burned in large pits dug in the soft limestone rock, and the ashes used to fertilize the land. Fans are now in constant use, much to our [annoyance] as we are frequently requested to write something in English upon them, which favour pleases them very much.

In the afternoon we saw a procession of the seven princes and their attendants issuing from the temple occupied by the Commodore. An interview had just been held, and they were now taking their

---

[113] Besides the four commissioners and their secretary, Mantarō Matsuzaki, the two new members, Mineshige Tsuzuki (d. 1858) and Seitarō Takenouchi, comptroller of the revenues were now added.

departure.[114] Each, according to rank, [was] carried in his sedan chair
with latticed windows, and followed by a select body of his retainers,
crier proceeding in front, calling out the name and rank of the prince.
In the rear of each body of retainers were servants carrying lacquered
boxes hung on poles, supported on their shoulders, containing changes
of garments. Behind the sedan chairs were pike and standard bearers,
the latter having their flags confined in black covers.

As the third counsellor[115] passed, he looked out of the window of
his sedan and smiled and bowed to us, which courtesy we, of course,
returned. I remembered him well, as having proved himself on former
occasions of festivity as quite a jovial character. During these proceedings the inhabitants of the town were grovelling to the very earth in
abject respect for their august presence.

JUNE 20TH

SINCE my last visit to the town, I have been on the opposite side;
ascended the hills and walked through the country; enjoyed from the
heights a fine view of the town and harbour, looking down upon the
deck of our ship which lay close by the foot of the declivity; and then
turned inland and soon lost our way among the small paths lined
on each side by a thick growth of trees and brushwood interspersed
with honeysuckle, wild roses, and various other kinds of flowers
which made the atmosphere fragrant with their odors.

Now and then we would pass some of the field labourers of both
sexes, on their way home after the day's toil, with their implements
of husbandry in their hands—a swarthy, hard-working race, but
cheerful. Then again, we would suddenly find ourselves in the cultivated grounds where they would be still at work, and the women
would cry out 'Ohio' (How are you?),[116] repeat the word 'America,'
and laugh good-humoredly. We discovered a grove [of] cherry trees
on our way back, and immediately climbed up among them and commenced making the best of our time, as such opportunities did not
offer every day. They were the small rum cherry, black and sharp-
tasting.

---

[114] 'After a succession of daily conferences,
which continued from the 8th to the 17th of
June, a mutual agreement was finally ad-
justed. . . . In regard to the various disputed
points of detail not specified in the treaty.'
For additional regulations, *see:* THE EXPEDI-
TION OF AN AMERICAN SQUADRON. V. 1, pp.
479-81.

[115] Masayoshi Izawa, lord of Mimasaku.

[116] *Ohayo*, pronounced as *Ohio* means 'Good
morning' in Japanese.

We spent the day in endeavouring to beat round the Island, but in consequence of light head winds and strong currents, failed. The night proving rainy and blowy, hove to under top sails. At daylight filled away, made sail, and stood for B——— rock, distant from Y——— thirty miles, and on our course for Simoda.

At about eight A.M, passed the Rock and made a number of Islands ahead.

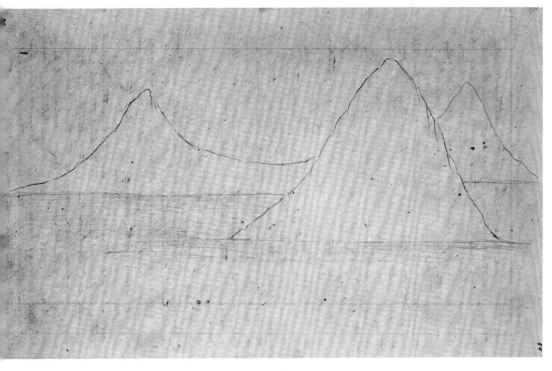

16 *Shimoda Bay*

In the course of our walk, the sun being very hot and the wind shut out by the woods, we sat down near a deserted lookout station on the edge of a cliff, though tall trees grew round us, and here smoked our pipes; and whilst gazing out upon the sea dotted with junks and here and there a small island near the coast, we—that is, Breese and myself—passed the time singing songs, humming tunes, and talking of what we would do on our return home. Very pleasant themes, which the length[en]ing shadows cast by the setting sun warned us, could not last long; so, retracing our steps and gathering flowers by the way, we returned on board, much invigorated by our walk and each bearing in his hand a large bunch of sweet-smelling flowers, conspicuous among them all being a species of *lile de l'eau*, some white and others pink, but both very fragrant and handsome.

JUNE 21ST

THIS day the bazaar was held on shore in one of their temples. The display of goods was small, and the prices exorbitant. I myself purchased but little. In the afternoon I strolled through the town endeavouring to pick up something either curious or pretty, but did not succeed; and when at sundown the officers gathered together near the landing it was laughable to see the multitude of useless articles which had been purchased for the want of something better. Sometimes one would have procured a bottle, tray, or cup which matched that possessed by another. In that case they would toss up to see who would have both, and I expect there are many who will find it difficult to stow their trumpery aboard ship.

The Commodore gave an entertainment to the seven Japanese counsellors and princes the other evening on board the *Mississippi*. On that occasion they brought with them over a hundred and twenty attendants. Some of them were quite young, being the sons of princes; and one in particular, a fine little fellow, drew very well and evidently liked cake, from the quantity he consumed. They were entertained by the Ethiopian band on the *Powhatan* and appeared to enjoy themselves very much. On the departure of each prince, a blue light was burned or rocket fired, which caused considerable astonishment among the natives.

Thus ended the last display of the Japan Expedition, which is now fast drawing to a close. A few days more and we will have set sail for China and will, in all probability, never see this country again or its peculiar people, who at one moment present to you some trait of an enlightened nation, and at another, one, found only among half-civilized people.

JUNE 30TH

QUIETLY have we been gliding on, since our departure from port, over the gently ruffled ocean. The rustling of our canvas stilled by the light wind and motionless in their expanded form propel us towards the sunny south, leaving the fogs and gales behind. The sun now shines hotly through the day, whilst its more tempered rays of evening, gilding the western horizon, tempt us to seek the deck and there reclining or sitting on the tafferel enjoy the quiet beauty of the scene and the refreshing influences of the cooling breeze.

As the departing beams of the setting sun become less and less distinct, and the golden hue of the clouds grows fainter and fainter in the west, and twilight gathers round us with all its soothing tranquility of feeling, one by one the little stars appear overhead and twinkle and twinkle and glimmer in their distant spheres. The crescent moon now rises into sight, and, giving forth its pale, clear light on the rippling ocean beneath, moves quietly on its pathless track in the heavens. The night reigns supreme in all its silent and impressive majesty. And now the dew begins to fall upon the deck, and the night wind is heavy with refreshing moisture.

Now one by one the officers disappear from the deck, some to read, some to enjoy their cigars, and others to seek repose before the approaching watch. The watch on deck have played their rough game, sung their song, or spun their yarn; and now, wrapping themselves in their pea-jackets, pick out the softest plank they can find and, with a coil of rigging for a pillow, there and then turn in for a nap. The officer of the deck paces up and down his monotonous round; the man at the wheel stands gazing up at the sails, now and then turning a spoke of the wheel to bring the ship up to her course, or to keep her from the wind as her head comes to one-third; the lookout stands at his post gazing out upon the trackless waters around him and passes the call as the halfhour bell strikes the time of night.

Not a sound breaks the stillness of the night, except the occasional flapping of a sail or the ripple of a wave parted at the bows, the foam on its surface glistening in the moon's ray. Silence reigns supreme. Nature sleeps upon the ocean in all its [sic] beauty of repose—in the clear sky above, in waters beneath—wrapt in the somber mantle of night.

Once more we commemorate the day upon the ocean. This time last year we were bound round the Cape of Good Hope, and now we are off the coast of Japan—next year, where will we be? Time only can tell: Perhaps (shall I say it?) homeward bound. But this is looking too much into the future, and raising hopes which may never come to pass.

We have now been out some eight days, during which time we have not had over twenty four hours' fair wind. This was on the day of departure from Simoda, and was followed by the southwest monsoons which, it appears, this year extend much further to the northward than usual. We first made a long tack to the southward until, arriving in the latitude of the islands of Loo Choo, we went about. We were then about four hundred miles to the westward of Loo Choo, and two hundred to the eastward of the Bonins.

Once more we are near the Japanese Islands, and about thirty miles off from the Island of [Kikai][117] and have experienced this afternoon the usual indications noticed on nearing an island, such as sudden squalls of wind and rain, the former changing its direction three out of four points either way with great rapidity. Our position on the chart places us about half-way between the port left (Simoda) and the port to which we are bound (Kelung on the northwest end of the Island of Formosa).

Having now been for some time out of both fresh provisions and cigars, comforts which add considerably to the agreeability of a passage, we long for fair breeze to shorten the way over this uncertain portion of the ocean. Fresh provisions we have seen but little since leaving Loo Choo. The men have lived entirely on salt rations, excepting fish and turtle occasionally. Officers and men use lime-water as an anti-scorbutic, and it has proved effectual.

This is the typhoon season, and we shall be at sea nearly to its close; so that if we escape it will be very fortunate, especially as both our present suite of sails and running gear are very old and worn out. Hardly a watch but some important rope parts, which would not answer in heavy weather. However, we hope for the best; and if our

[117] Devil's Island on the shore of Satsuma, where the priest Shunkwan was banished after he plotted to overthrow the powerful clan of the Tairas. For the famous *No* play SHUNKWAN, *see:* Arthur Waley, THE NO PLAYS OF JAPAN, 1922. pp. 229-35.

old sails are split we can find new ones, which we do not use now, being desirous to preserve them for our next cruising ground.

JULY 5TH

AND the 9th day out. I wonder much where the store-ship *Supply* is at this present time.[118] When we arrive in port, I shall mark down her track on a chart with her own, and find them both, no doubt, much alike. Last night in my first watch we sighted the Island of [Miyako] ahead, and went about. Tacking again in the morning, we have been standing along the chain of islands which extends here in a southwest and northeast direction. They are six or eight in number, the largest of which, [Nishiomote], has a mountain in the middle 5000 ft. high,[119] but it has been enveloped in clouds most of the day.

8 p.m. The night is clear, the moon shines brightly and the wind light from southeast. Down to leeward the positions of the several islands are indicated by heavy dark masses of clouds, which remain suspended over them like a pall.

We are now in the northeasterly current which prevails here like our own Gulf Stream, sweeping up the coast of China, through the Loo Choo Group, and up along the coast of Japan. To its influence we are no strangers, having encountered it frequently before. Its strength is now about a mile and half an hour, and against us.

Notre voyage des découvert once accomplished, we will have the satisfaction of knowing that our keel has ploughed this portion of the ocean in every direction, and that our chart will rectify many mistakes, clear up many doubts, and show the position of rocks and islands heretofore unknown. In other words, that our long absence from fresh beef and civilization, though the cause of present discomfort, will ultimately prove a source of satisfaction to all concerned therein, and the same may be said of most of the squadron. The difference in the case of the steamers being that they, being much more in port and making generally direct passages, have been able on every occasion to clear the market of all superfluities prior to our arrival—a very important advantage when the desired articles can only be procured in very limited quantities. At present they are at Loo Choo, concluding

---

[118] 'On the second day out the *Supply* disappeared, and was not seen again until she entered the harbor of Kelung, Formosa, on the 21st of July, ten days after the arrival at that place of the *Macedonian,* which had made the run from Simoda in about twelve days. . . .' THE EXPEDITION OF AN AMERICAN SQUADRON. v. 1. p. 498.

[119] Furumidake, 1700 ft. high.

a treaty with the regent or king of that group[120] and we shall not see them again until our arrival in Hongkong some two months hence, where a final separation will take place, some remaining on the station to represent the Stars and Stripes, whilst others will bear away home-ward bound—our ship, however, will not be of that number. Still, our day will come in due time.

---

[120] A compact between the United States and the authorities of Loo Choo was signed at Napha on July 11, 1854.

Breese's Description
of the Formosa
Coal Field

JULY 10TH

A T last we have arrived off our port, this being the evening of the fifteenth day of our passage; and well satisfied are we all that it has come to a termination, for although two weeks is but a short time to be at sea, still circumstances alter cases, and in our case this is but a temporary stopping place. And glad am I that it is so, as we cannot expect to see anything of much interest, or at least not to compensate for a much longer delay in receiving news from home, our last dates being as far back as the first of December. Since then many changes of more or less importance have, no doubt, taken place, and the mind becomes anxious to know what they may be—good or evil. Hope delayed makes the heart sick.

Though the winds have not been propitious to us, still the weather has been generally very pleasant, and the warm day succeeded by a moonlight night, the tranquil sea, and soft south wind [which] have all combined to render the time agreeable. Now and then when in the neighbourhood of islands we have experienced a rain squall or sudden shift of wind to vary the monotony, but, once more on the open sea, the wind would return to the old quarter, and day and night be as before.

I remember on a particular mid-watch when the ship was heeling over to a freshening breeze and the whole heavens were resplendent with [the] clear light of the moon, the clouds began to gather along the horizon in dark, heavy masses, which, as they rose higher and higher until nearly overhead, became separated and detached, assuming the form of semi-circles. Each are extending over a wide space—some curves one way and some another—and the moon's rays shining in between them, made the whole have the appearance of an immense cage. Gradually, however, the lower clouds banked up in denser

E

masses in all directions, and vivid lightning commenced playing along the horizon, both to windward and down to leeward; and then followed the low, muttering sound of rolling thunder.

Faster and stronger came the wind squalls, accompanied by a few drops of rain. The moon had now disappeared from view, and all was darkness, except when the heavens were illuminated by the glare of the lightning, revealing for a brief instant the ponderous piles of clouds looming in all their majesty one above the other. Having handed all the light sails, the watch stood prepared for the coming change.

Suddenly the wind lulled, the heavy canvas flapped listlessly against the masts, but only for a moment. A bright flash, a heavy peal, and the squall was upon us! Down came the wind and rain, and over on her lee side careened the ship, until, gaining an impetus from the power of the wind, she rushed like an arrow through the water, whilst the low flapping of our mainsail, as its widespread folds were furled to the breeze, but added to the confusion of the scene.

Again the wind suddenly ceases, then shifts and comes out astern, and before the ship can be brought to her course it is ahead, and has taken us aback.

Hard up! And our swift progress through the water enables us to fill on the same tack. Once more the squall thickens round us, and the rain falls in slanting, blinding sheets.

See the halliards clear, for it blows a gale!

In the wind, let her go off, flatten in—all full again, meet her! Crash! goes the thunder overhead—that flash must have been very near.

Flap, sound the sails against the masts—what will come next?

And now the rain ceases; the heavy clouds pass to leeward; the moon shines brighly overhead; the old wind springs up, and the squall is past. Like so many sons of Neptune, just risen from their watery element, the sailors shake their dripping clothes, and in obedience to the word of command climb aloft and loose the lighter sails to the breeze—and again the ship is clothed in her white suit from deck to truck.

Strike the bell eight, call the watch, tumble up below these—the watch is over!

And when relieved, each one goes below, and, turning in, is soon oblivious of wind and rain, thunder and lightning, and all the other changes of the elements.

The above is a rough out-line of Bruce, Waters &
myself cutting and eating pine apples under an old
china man's shed, after a long mornings walk through

17 *Eating Pineapples in a Shed*

12 at night. I had just dropped off into a pleasant slumber, having enjoyed the evening breeze until a short time previous on deck, when I was awakened by a great noise on deck and nearly rolled out of my bunk, the ship heeling over very much. The word was passed fore and aft for all hands to tumble up and shorten sail. A few moments and I was on deck, just in time to see the topsails clewed down to a very heavy squall which, it appears, had come up very unexpectedly, and proved to be the first of a numerous series which followed each other in succession during the night. We were very fortunate in having just cleared the islands, which gave us thirty miles sea room to work ship in.

In the morning when I turned out we were under topsails and courses running free. Keelung Island was close aboard, a small conical island four miles from the port, and looming up through the mist right ahead rose the high land of Formosa. Several heavy squalls obliged us to lay to until they cleared off, when, taking advantage of a lull, we stood in, taking on board a Chinese pilot; and before meridian were at anchor in the harbour of Keelung.

Capt. [N. Guerin], R. N., in command of a merchantman,[121] the—, visited this port some time ago and made a rough chart of the harbour, which answers all practical purposes, although incorrect in some respects. We will, however, give it a thorough survey before leaving.

The entrance is narrow with considerable high land all round. Proceeding up about a mile, it becomes narrow and shoals. Beyond this is the junk anchorage, opposite one end of the town, which is built upon the left bank off the harbour and extends upwards of a mile or more, consisting in most places of one, and, at most, of three streets running in a parallel direction.

The above is a rough outline of Breese, Watters, and myself, cutting and eating pineapples under an old Chinaman's shed, after a long morning's walk through the town in the hot sun, which had somewhat fatigued us; and we proposed and put into exectuion this method of refreshing ourselves, much to the gratification of the old stall-keeper and amusement of a large crowd of men and boys who encircled us during the operation, examining our dress and arms as great curiosities (as they were, no doubt, to them); the only objection to their

---

[121] 'Before the visit of the United States squadron to these seas, a French chart, constructed by Monsieur N. Guerin; Captaine de vaisseau, and published in Paris in 1848, was the most approved guide.' THE EXPEDITION OF AN AMERICAN SQUADRON. v. 1, p. 489.

presence being the difficulty we found in keeping their not over-clean hands off our white clothes.

We called on the Chief Mandarin[122] at his residence and were politely received by his son, the old man not being in. Refreshments were served, consisting of pop-corn rolls, tea, and cakes. I sat next to the young mandarin, and his pipe-bearer, standing between us, passed the brass narghile alternately to each, and I found the flavor very agreeable. We sat in the paved court or reception room, with a large crowd at the entrance (and partly in the room) gazing on in clamorous admiration. In the afternoon the mandarin[s] visited the ship, with which they were very much [pleased] and presented us with a bullock.

This afternoon landed a little above the ship, and visited a Chinese fortification, consisting of a solid stone bastion some fifteen feet in height and the same in thickness, with a breastwork extending along the front, pierced for larger guns at intervals, with loopholes between for musketry. At the present time there are no guns mounted. Like forts are erected near various quarters of the town, which is circled by a stone wall on the shore sides, some six feet in height, with bastions and loopholes at regular distances. Just now they are in daily fear of an attack from the rebels on the China side, and have, in consequence, they say, several hundred troops under arms, although in corroboration of the statement I have only seen a small encampment at one end of the town, containing perhaps a hundred or two armed men, two thirty-two pounders, and several jingals.

Their camp consists of about a dozen or so small tents, which after rain, the camp-ground being low, are nearly all afloat. The dress of the soldiers differs but little from the ordinary garments of the inhabitants, and their appearance is anything but prepossessing. Each tent is occupied by some dozen soldiers, sitting on straw which covers the ground, and generally eating boiled rice as a means of passing the time when not sleeping.

Their cannon are mounted upon heavy thick planks, placed edgewise and bolted together (also scored in the middle to receive the trunnions). Here and in an open court opposite the tosh house are all the ordinance of the town. The largest piece is a 68 pounder. They are constructed by the Chinese themselves and cast with the base.

---

[122] 'We were taken afterward to the house of a mandarin whose name is *Le-chu-ou,* and title *Hip-top,* said to be the chief mandarin of the place.' THE EXPEDITION OF AN AMERICAN SQUADRON. v. 1, p. 157.

…valesmen, I have only seen a small …
…nd of the town, containing perhaps a hundred or two armed
men, two thirty two pounders, and several jingals. their
camp consists of about a dozen or so small tents, which after
rain, the camp ground being low, are nearly all afloat.

18 *Military Camp in Keelung, Formosa*

The dress of the soldiers differs but little from the ordinary
garments of the inhabitants, and their appearance is any thing
but prepossessing — each tent is occupied by some dozen soldiers, sitting
on straw, which covers the ground, and generally eating boiled rice,
as a means of passing the time when not sleeping. their cannon

The streets of Keelung are a succession of arcades, with, for Chinese, very good ranges of shops on each side, and the pavements in front covered with a busy throng vending fruits and trinkets of every description and quality—except the best.

The whole presents a busy scene, which is the principal feature in all Chinese towns, caused in a great measure by the dense population inhabiting a small space; and when the streets are narrow, as in Canton, excepting [in] a few of the principal streets, the rush almost endangers personal safety.

The districts in which vegetables, fish, poultry, and fruit are sold present a very goodly array of the above-mentioned provisions. The pineapples are plentiful, also mangoes of a good quality; the sweet potatoes, especially the top ones, large; eggs, principally those of ducks. Bananas are scarce, the country being too hilly for them, [and] the same may be said of coconuts. The watermelons are excellent—not large, but with very thin rinds.

Continued our walk through the town, stopping now and then to examine the contents of the stores, or accepting the often-repeated invitation to walk in and take a pipe and cup of tea, on which occasions we would write in English for them, or draw a rough chart, showing the vessels' track and destination, with which they were very much pleased, many understanding the position of the countries, represented on the chart, very well.

Passing through and out by the opposite end of the town, followed a path leading by numerous paddy fields. Ascended the side of a hill by a stone-paved road, considerably out of repair, evidently from the effect of rains; and when on the summit enjoyed a fine view of the dark-green and hilly country, the town beneath and harbour beyond.

Here and there were immense mud-flats, marring the view with their moist dingy brown, and telling too truly by the miasmatic atmosphere which quivered above them, of disease and death to all foreign to the climate. Noticed several trees near-by whose [trunks] and twisted branches had grown together in a very singular manner.

Birds of a kind or kinds, that I had never seen before were singing and flitting about in every direction. Heavy clouds were gathering in the west, and the distant sound of thunder came muttering among the hills, and soon followed a refreshing shower of rain, which cleared off in a few minutes, giving the atmosphere a fresh elastic feeling, making the grass and herbage to glisten in their renewed vigor, and as the setting sun appeared from among the now scattered clouds, a half-circle rainbow appeared in view, close to us, adding beauty to the scene.

> 'A rainbow at night
> A sailor's delight.'

On our way back stopped at several farmhouses, where in every case our gallant bearing in encountering the dogs who invariably made hostile demonstrations towards us, caused the women, at least, to decamp, and left us masters of the household. But we generously forebore, and contented ourselves with an examination of the premises, and then left them to the rightful owners.

Retracing our steps through the town, were overtaken by the rain unexpectedly, and seated ourselves in consquence under a covered way, and whilst there a young Chinaman offered us in a pressing manner some rice cakes, which we as politely declined, having but little faith in their cul[inary] abilities. He then exchanged them for a handful of betelnut chews, but with no better success, as we preferred keeping our teeth white. But not to discourage him I presented him with a string of cash (Chinese money) for which he was very thankful, not having in all probability ever received a gift before in his life.

We did the same to an old man selling pineapples near-by, and they both followed us with pineapples in their hands for some distance, and were really very much disappointed because we would not accept them. We did not on this occasion, as before, endeavour to purchase chickens or ducks, feeling no desire to stand amidst an admiring crowd with sword on one side and pistol on the other and cheapen[123] fowls, so took a *sampan* (native boat) and returned to the ship.

Several of the officers, this day, visited a coal mine about a mile from the town. They found it of easy access and apparently good quality. The mandarins state that the junks load with this useful, and, in this part of the world, scarce article, at a port eighty miles to the southward of this place. We wanted to form a party, and, assisted by a Chinese guide, make a land excursion to the mines, but on inquiry we found that on account of the barbarous tribes—and, as they say here, also cannibals—which infest the country, none of the Chinese would show us the way; so here the expedition ends, no doubt.

We visited this port with two objects in view; namely, to obtain coal (which we have at least found) and to discover if there were any prisoners upon the islands—unfortunate seamen cast away on this

---

[123] Archaic, used in the sense 'to beat down the price of'.

inhospitable land and doomed either to death or slavery. But on this point we have been unable to gain any information, as the Chinese have but little intercourse with the savage tribes, that we can discover, holding but an insecure footing themselves and liable to attacks from their formidable enemies at any moment. This is in every sense an unknown island to civilized nations, and years will in all probability lapse before any determined steps will be taken to explore it to any great extent.

Since our arrival mandarins have visited the ship, but today the Governor or Chief Mandarin visited the ship, accompanied by two others of the same grade, but lower on the scale, and attended by an escort of ragged soldiers, bearing pipes and red umbrellas. There are seven grades of mandarins in China.[124]

The Governor of this place is of the third grade; those who accompanied him, of the fifth and sixth respectively. He was a tall, slim, dark-complexioned person, inferior in personal appearance to one of the others, who was very well formed, and also of a prepossessing bearing. Everything excited his curiosity that he saw, as a ship of this size has never visited this harbour before, and [he] showed great pleasure in being saluted with *three guns* (that being a Chinese salute). The Captain today presented him unofficially—that is, through the purser[125]—with a number of ship's knives, scissors, and other articles of interest, as curiosities to them. This treatment has placed fresh provisions and fruits at our command in much to be desired quantities, which we all willingly take advantage of, for I learn today that we have a hundred men on board more or less affected by scurvy, so that a change from salt to fresh diet has become an absolute necessity.

I have since learned that there are nine grades of mandarins, and that the Governor is of the 4th grade and the other two of the 6th and 7th, wearing blue, white, and yellow buttons, or top balls on their conical hats, which mark denotes the grade of the wearer.

JULY 16TH

THIS afternoon, the weather being pleasant, I went on shore more for exercise than observation, but who can visit a foreign people or a strange place without seeing something to attract his attention? And such was the case with myself on this occasion.

---

[124] Not seven, but nine, as later corrected, known as *Chiu-p'in*.

[125] Purser Richard T. Allison.

We landed at the lower end of the town, passed through the principal street, encountering the usual quantity of noise and confusion, much of which emanated from the numerous small gambling shops which are to be met with in every Chinese town. Passed the *hongs*, and then the graveyards, or continuous burying place, which reaches nearly down to the water's edge, and here we saw an exhumed coffin among a collection of graves, several of which were new. It consisted of the portion of a trunk of a tree hollowed out, cut off at one side, and boarded over. The excavation made for its reception in the ground is so shallow that I noticed in several instances the ends of the coffins protruding from out the raised mounds. We next came to the wooden bridge, supported on rough stone columns, which extends across a wide mud-bottomed stream, that is almost dry at low water, and again entered the town. One of the first persons I encountered was the Governor on his visit aboard. The fat old gentleman was fanning himself most energetically, and gave us a familiar nod, by way of recognition, making signs for us to enter at the same time, which we politely declined, and continued on.

Stopped at the tosh house and saw a number of women in white (their mourning dress) performing their devotions by prostrating themselves before the image, burning paper and waving it up and down, as they repeated their incantations. On each side of the altar there was a wooden figure of hideous aspect, one red and the other blue—gods of Peace and War.

As usual, an admiring crowd followed us wherever we went, much to our an[noyance], but we bore it as a necessary evil, and thought, in extenuation, how a Chinese would be treated similarly situated in our country.

Returning, we stepped into a house to observe the operation of one woman pulling out by means of a twisted cord the superfluous hair on the neck of another. It was very skillfully performed, although our presence evidently embarrassed them. We reach the landing by sunset and found officers and men bargaining for provisions of every kind, which are now much cheaper than when we first arrived.

JULY 17TH

ANOTHER day has passed and still no signs of the *Supply*. This is her 21st day out, and yet, though we made the passage in fifteen day[s], we expected to find the store ship in port on our arrival.

*I have since learned that there are nine grades of Mandarins, & that the Governor is of the 4th Grade & the other two of the 6th and 7th. A Blue white and Yellow button or top balls on their Conical hats, which mark denotes the grade of the Maser.

38

19 *A Mandarin*

I[126] started this morning at half past four in the cutter for the famous mines of Formosa, from which so much benefit to the whole world (some few speculating Amer[ican] merchants) is to be derived, and for which I, poor fellow, was turned out of my ship to incommode some and benefit others. But, however, off we started: Mr. Jones,[127] the chaplain, under whose favored [tutelage] I am at present; the purser, an amateur; two Chinese guides, who to serve Mammon forgot their master; and a Chinese interpreter. Before going on, it would perhaps better to say that I was 'put out', to use a ladies' phrase, and this may, in fact, account for the gloomy narrative which follows. And perhaps still more better [sic] would it be should I tell my grievances, that my account might be looked over more leniently than it would otherwise have been.

To begin with, I was told that I need not make any preparations as regards chow-chow for the next day (today), as they—the purser and chaplain—had prepared all. And as everyone knows that travelling in an open boat on a hot day on an empty stomach is contrary to all the laws of nature, as soon as I was dressed, I looked around for my break-fast. Not having received any invitation to partake of one which was cooking in fine style, notwithstanding it was so early in the morning, I began to feel queer and thought of being slighted. Thinking that if I did not try for my *déjeuner* no one would for me, a lucky idea struck me as I thought. 'Perhaps Mr. Jones might have some things to be at-tended to (although the matter and arrangement had been thoroughly canvassed and arranged the previous day) and I ought to go in the cabin (where the breakfast was going) and find out,' which I did.

Oh, sorrowful moment! There were but two plates on the table and the purser, standing by, waiting for the chaplain to sit down and com-mence his attack upon the nice viands displayed before him.

I drew myself up to my full height, five feet ten without shoes—not 'in my stocking feet', as I once expressed it before some ladies who were dreadfully shocked at the expression—and modestly asked if the chaplain was dressed.

Receiving a polite negative in reply I withdrew, fully determined to sacrifice myself to the raw pork and moldy hardtack of the boat crew, and had hardly got more than a few paces on my way when—oh, luck! —a twang went through my bowels, which, followed by others in

---

[126] The handwriting changes here and is that of Kidder Randolph Breese, who was tempo-rarily attached to the *Macedonian* during her cruise to Formosa.

[127] Reverend George Jones (1800–70), naval chaplain and author.

quick succession, soon reduced me to the idea of filling up that awful void and causing me to place, more than ever, my implicit reliance upon the old adage that Nature abhors a vacuum. I perfectly agreed with Nature. I called the steward, explained my situation, received his commiseration with a sigh as he told me that he was so sorry and why had I not told him before, etc. and asked him to get me a cup of tea while I took a stroll on deck and examined the fittings of my boat.

I could not have been on deck five minutes when up he came (the steward) and told me my tea was ready. I thought he might have brought it up, only a cup of tea, and I was going to be gone in the hot, broiling sun for the whole day. 'Well,' I thought, 'that, better than nothing,' and down I went to the pantry. Imagine my surprise, my delight, my ecstasy at the sight—and I really believe the good steward enjoyed my delight as much as I did the sight. There was a plate with a breast, a back, two legs, two wings, side bones, etc. of a chicken—in fact, I might say there was a whole chicken—and near it some fresh pork, devilled. When I left the pantry the teapot was nearly dry and nothing remained of the chicken but the bones.

How well I felt! No more rumblings, everything well stowed and in good trim. As old Dick Chapman would say, 'A child might play with me,' or, as the Emperor of China might remark, 'I have breakfast and now let all the world.....'

I was met on my ascent on deck by a cabin boy with, 'Mr. Jones wishes you to take breakfast with him.'

'Better late than [n]ever,' thought I. But, said I, with a perfect air of *bienséance*, I had breakfasted. Sproston's remark about pineapples—the difference existing between nowadays and formerly—has quite sobered me, and I will try now and proceed to the real object of the expedition.

The highest mandarin on shore, after having taken a second sober thought, declined to furnish guides to show the mines to the *Fanquis* [foreigner?] for fear the news of it might reach the ears of the authorities in China and he be deprived of his button for his civility. But he must have much mistaken the great American nation (which the ship here represents), did he think that we would give it up so, particularly with the *corps scientifique* on board, of which Mr. Jones is the head, and I having all under my protection (that is, I wear a sword and revolver constantly to prevent any unpleasant occurence taking place, such as being broiled and eaten or led away into captivity, perhaps to work some of the very mines about which so much interest is displayed).

However, through the aid of the Captain's steward, a Chinaman, guides were procured (I believe also at the connivance of the mandarin). They came on board at dusk last evening, talked mysteriously, and said that in two hours they would take us to the long-desired-to-be-seen mines so near the water. They insisted upon being disguised as sea men, which was soon done, and as they were clean, could not have been recognised by their best friend as natives of Keelung.

Equipped as I have described, we shoved off at half past four, early daylight. It was a delightful morning, cool and pleasant, just breeze enough ahead to ripple the water and not to stop the headway of the boat, and a fair tide, being everything to make one comfortable and happy. Being on this occasion a Cavalier and feeling myself as such and thinking that I had been treated as one (cavalierly), I lighted my cigar and wrapped myself in my own thought[s], they following the motions of my cigar smoke, [which], at first a confused mass and then breaking out and taking various forms, gradually disappeared (what shall I say to wind up this beautifully poetical idea? Shall it be the blue vault of heaven? No. I've hit it!) like snow before a March wind.

This must do now, as I've started at last in my story, until tomorrow, when probably my *observations* will be noted down and, I hope, handed down to posterity as they certainly ought to, and when Commodore Perry sees this book which I shall certainly recommend him to do, he will acknowledge the truth of it. Won't Johnny rave at my carelessness—Bloss !!!![128]

The foregoing is Breese's account of his expedition to the coal mine of Formosa, the successful issue of which is a great source of satisfaction to all, as it has placed beyond a doubt the fact of the existence of extensive veins of coal upon the Island, of easy access, and from all appearances of good quality. When we consider that not three hundred miles from this port (Shanghai) coal is selling for $60 a ton,[129] it is truly astonishing that more notice has not been taken of the existence of it here, and [a] depot for the useful article established.

It only shows clearly how much yet remains to be discovered and explored of the seaboard of China, a country inhabited by a people differing in every respect from other nations. Their manner of living in

[128] End of Breese's handwriting.

[129] From the report of Chaplain Jones to Commodore Perry: '. . . .by Captain Abbot's direction, to purchase all that was sufficiently large for our purposes, which I did at $16 for each hundred piculs. They demanded $20. The Hip-toy had said that we ought to give but $12, and $12 is probably the regular price; but we thought it cheap at $16, and were glad to get it at that. . . .' THE EXPEDITION OF AN AMERICAN SQUADRON. V. 2, p. 162.

particular, combined with the unhealthiness [sic] of the climate, will always be a great drawback to any but a slow and gradually increasing intercourse with them.

A few remarks might now be appropriately made concerning the history of the Island to the present day, which will solve the cause of many difficultes still existing to prevent for intercourse on their part with foreigners, and not the least will be found to have originated with Europeans themselves.

For the great misfortune attending the propagation of civilization and Christianity among heathens is that the class of foreigners with whom they first come in contact with [sic] are actuated only by motives of gain, irrespective of the method by which it is obtained, and which is generally, as proved by history, an unlawful one enforced by men who have been obliged to leave their own country from misconduct or from incompetency to restrict themselves within the bounds of propriety. In other words, they are but adventurers.

These are followed in time by a class of men of higher standing, at least in the commercial world, and who reflect all due credit upon the standing of enlightened nations as compared with semi-barbarians. But, fortunately, for the rapid advance of social intercourse, the pernicious effects of the first remain, a lasting evidence of the good faith on the part of those who, uninvited and undesired, have endeavoured to establish themselves in the homes of another people. When such is the state of affairs, what can be expected on the part of those thus maltreated but distrust [and] enmity?

Look at the behavior of the Spaniards and Portuguese in the Americas! Grasping avarice glossed over by a shadow of Christian chivalry governed their every act; the conduct of the Dutch, a selfish, sordid race, whose ruling motive is self-benefit and for self only. And yet these nations first visited and colonized China and Japan! What worse foundation for a future superstructure?

Formosa is a large island off the Province of Yokien [Fu-chien] China, from which it is separated by a channel from 90 to 120 miles in breadth. Its length is about 250 miles by 50 or so in width. It was the last conquest made [in] the present Tartar dynasty, and even now, it is only a conquest by name, as the Chinese are restricted to a very small part of the Island. Vessels have now and then been wrecked upon its inhospitable shores, [and] the fates of all have been death or captivity.

In the 17th century the Dutch had a colony here, but were in time expelled by the pirate chief. Their desire for gain and method of obtaining it, at the same time neglecting to keep the colony in a proper state of defense, combined to produce their expulsion. It was here also that they met with retributive justice from the Japanese for some unauthorized act on their part towards the crews of several junks belonging to that nation. The Dutch had a factory and garrison at this very port. Coxinja[130] was the name of the pirate chief who drove them off the Island, not before, however, (and it may be said to their credit in this instance) they had propagated Christian principles extensively among the natives; but all signs of such a desirable reformation have disappeared long ere this present period.

[130] Dutch ruled over a large portion of Formosa from 1624–61, but they were ousted from the island by Kokusenya (Chinese Chêng Ch'êng-kung, 1624–62), the son of a Chinese pirate by a Japanese mother. But his rule was short-lived, and the island passed in 1683 under the control of the Chinese Government, which retained it until its cession to Japan in 1895.

The History
of
Formosa

JULY 20TH

THIS afternoon the joyful sight of a full-rigged ship hove in sight off the harbour, when we instantly fired a gun, supposing, as it is without doubt, the long-looked-for *Supply* at last hove in sight, having prolonged the passage ten days beyond our time. As I think I have before mentioned, the day and particulary the night after our arrival we had a succession of tremendous squalls which were generally considered as the effects of a typhoon coming over the hills and then blowing off the coast, and as the *Supply* was very light, we felt somewhat anxious about her, which feeling gained strength from her non-appearance as day succeeded day. The wind dying away has prevented her getting [in] this evening, but the morning will, no doubt, find her at anchor, and I hope two or three days and we will be off for still more southern climes, although as we have not had the thermometer below 84°, even at night whilst in port, most persons think that we are near enough the line.

Yesterday the Chinese and rebels had an encounter some 40 miles from here which ended in the total discomfiture of the former, who have made this port in their warlike junks and have been saluting the mandarins of the port, on their official visits on board, with a red cotton umbrella over the heads and a pipe-bearer by their sides.

The above is a representation of a Chinese war junk.[131] The numerous parti-coloured ensigns represent the province to which they belong or the troops they have on board. The whole, or *tout ensemble*, is a correct representation of the mimicry of war, caused by the Celestials' utter want of military knowledge in either land or sea engagements. Collectively, in time of action they behave like brave children, but,

---

[131] There is no illustration but a blank space.

individually, (particularly the Tartar soldiers) have often shown a degree of bravery of example; for instance, in the wars with the English, when the superiority of enlightened tactics and foreign implements of destruction had carried the day against native opposition, imperfectly and ill directed, they have been frequently known to deliberately cut their throats in the presence of the victorious enemy, or drown themselves in the river, the latter being the usual method of self-destruction resorted to by the mandarins or highest officers. If their wives and children happened to be within reach, they also destroy them, and frequently have the English been eye-witnesses of such barbarous acts of self-immolation.

Yesterday a crowd of Chinese attacked one our of boat's crews, who had been trading with them, and I am sorry to say no doubt cheating them, for Jack afloat is not the gallant tar he is supposed to be by landsmen. Such cases certainly exist, but they are the exceptions, not the rule. The coxswain of the boat shot one of them through both legs (fortunately for him, a flesh wound). His wounds were dressed on board, and, as he was proved to have been a non-combatant at the time, a present of $5 and a quantity of ship's drilling were given him— a temporary balm to his injured feelings. At his own desire a Chinese boat brought him off this morning to have his wounds redressed. He made the doctor[132] a present of some chickens and eggs as a token of gratefulness for his attention, I suppose. We have shot many alongside with small shot for attempting to smuggle liquors aboard, and having no covering on generally, the discharges have cut them up considerably and checked in a great measure this nefarious action. Effective means must be resorted to where milder ones are inadequate.

TUESDAY, JULY 25TH

With a light wind aft, and a perfectly smooth sea, with steering sails set low and aloft, we are now quietly gliding down the passage between Formosa and the coast of China. The lofty rolling hills of the former are now in sight on our port or left hand. In the distance, now and then, a large junk is seen; their large, square sails and cumbrous hulls looming up like line of battle-ships along the horizon. We might with reason expect to encounter in these latitudes the southwest monsoons, which, with a current ahead, would make our progress

---

[132] Dr. James S. Gilliam.

very tedious; so that every hour this wind continues is so much gained.

Sunday morning [July 23rd] we up anchor and stood out of the *Supply* in port coaling, and that by stealth, the Chinese junks employed for the purpose of conveying the coal from the mines—distant about five miles—refusing to deliver it alongside, except at night. She will, however, have sailed by this time, bound direct to Hongkong.

Watters is attached to her, leaving me the only representative remaining of the old Princeton's Passed Union's Mess,[133] which at one time consisted of eight members. Now they are scattered to every part of the globe and may not meet again in life. Such cases occur every day in the service, and illustrate the truth of Chateaubrian[d]'s sentiments which I have quote[d] in his own language: 'How many times has this since occurred to my mind, and often has it since been my lot to witness the dispersion of friends with whom I have spent many happy hours. The fragility of all human ties has often warned me against attaching myself too closely to any object.'

An unexpected supply of Manila cheroots enables us to pass the time very agreeably now, in connection with an agreeable book, an instructive one, perforce, as we are somewhat reduced in our literary lore. Now and then you even see an officer beguiling his time with the *Naval Register*, and ours are two years old at that. It can't be to mark off the vacancies, as they happen too seldom, [so] the object must be their listlessness with the thermometer at ninety odd.

JULY 27TH, '54

SINCE last writing we have experienced one of those changes incidental to these seas at this time of the year. During the night of the 25th indications of bad weather made their appearance. Heavy masses of clouds banked up along the northern horizon, which lay on our weather quarter, and the wind commenced gradually freshening. At daylight I came on watch and found all steering sails off the ship.

Soon after, we were running off twelve knots with reduced sail. The whole sky was now covered with jagged wind-riven clouds, and the barometer was falling fast. In consequence, reefed down. In the forenoon watch, reduced sail to close-reefed topsails and foresail,

---

[133] Probably 'Princeton' here refers to the *Princeton* which was built in Philadelphia between 1842–43, but as far as I can ascertain, neither Sproston nor Watters had been asigned to the *Princeton*.

and kept away dead before it, steering south. Strong squalls of wind
swept past us with shortening intervals between; and a gale, perhaps
typhoon, was from all indications inevitable. The order was passed
to furl the fore-topsail. At this time the watch below were at dinner.

Suddenly the cry came from aloft, 'Man overboard!' Everyone
instantly rushed on deck. The ship was being brought by the wind;
the buoy overboard, the life-crew were clearing away the boat. But
it was all useless. The lifeless body of the unfortunate man[134] was seen
slowly sinking forever beneath the foaming waves, which had closed
above him already, as the ship on her impetuous course swept swiftly
by. He had been out on the weather fore-topsail yard-arm, and whilst
speaking to the captain of the top suddenly disappeared off the yard,
fell across the fore channels and bounded overboard. His fall was from
a height of about eighty feet. He was a young man and a good top
hand. Today you would not know that it had ever occurred. His name
will be struck off the watch bill, and that's the last of him.

In the evening sent down the topgallant masts, and took in all
sail except the close-reefed main-topsail and close-reefed foresail.
We were now abreast of the Pescadores,[135] off which there is an
immense shoal extending for miles and miles with not more than from
five to twenty fathoms water. The sea was a beautiful light green
colour, sparkling with the foam of the rolling waves, and covered with
the misty spray blown in wide sheets from the summits of the cresting
billows, which, as they lifted their white tops to the strong blast,
were twisted into graceful yet fantastical forms, and then, as if by a
mighty effort of the gale, riven assunder and scattered far and wide.
Still these are dangerous shoals, and I was glad once more to see the
water assume its natural deep blue color.

At night the gale freshened and blew very heavily, hauling at the
same time to the westward. The night was as black as Erebus, the wind
roared so as to hush the rolling thunder; the vivid lightning flashed all
round us, making the darkness in the intervals total blackness, besides
which the ship was now headed off to southeast, and Formosa Island
lay under our lee. Still we had every reason to suppose that body or
center of the typhoon had passed astern of us. From this acknowledged

---

[134] Captain Abbot to Commodore Perry
dated August 26, 1854: '. . . .I lament to have
to state that on the 26th ultimo, while shortening sail in the border of the typhoon spoken of,
Charles Wentworth, an excellent man, a
foretop-man, fell from the fore-topsail yard
overboard, and sunk immediately, first stiking

his head and breast upon the iron work of the
lower studding-sail swinging-boom, splitting
his head open, which must have killed him
instantly.' THE EXPEDITION OF AN AMERICAN
SQUADRON. V. 2, p. 144.

[135] Hōkō Rettō.

theory, and, consequently, we expected it would expend its force during the night, which it did, and though morning broke with a moderate gale, we have since sent up our poles and are gradually making sails; but the remainder of the passage will no doubt be made against strong southwest monsoons, which will take a week or more to accomplish. Land is just reported from aloft. It may be the south end of Formosa.

JULY 28TH

AFTER writing the above I went on deck to stand my watch. Along the weather horizon immense black semicircular clouds with a livid sky beneath. We thought they were coming up, but they did not. Passing off to leeward, they disappeared in sheets of lightning, and left us with a steady monsoon blowing right ahead of course. Put ship about with her head west southwest and, during the night under-reefed topsails cleeved down to several heavy squalls, one of which caught us aback.

During this day the weather has been generally moderate until this afternoon, when returning [to] the deck for a few minutes, a rain squall passed over, to which I took in the light sails, judging from appearances that it contained wind, but it did not. Shortly after, another black mass came slowly down upon us, but this time I held on until when it was very near us, then I noticed that it was acted upon by more than one current of air, as it would first take one direction and then another, and also that the lower edges drooped and peaked. This in particular arrested my attention, and, as I supposed, not without reason, for in a minute or two these drooping points elongated, the water beneath them became greatly agitated, and, lastly, some half-dozen small spiral columns formed themselves, being so many water-spouts. Not a moment was lost in getting sail off the ship, which was hardly accomplished when the squall struck us with force. Kept away just in time to prevent ship being taken aback. Down came the rain in a perfect deluge; and when the squall was passed, we all locked as if we had been overboard.

EVENING OF THE LAST OF JULY

WE are now three hundred miles from Manila, having made only one hundred and thirty miles in the last three days. This is not very encouraging, but I hope a week's perseverance, with even this indifferent luck, will find us in our destined port. We have not only the disadvantage of a hard wind, but also a very changeable one. One moment it is nearly calm; the next, black clouds gather along the horizon, and come down slowly upon the ship, and for a few minutes you are careening over to a heavy squall under reduced sail, with a blinding rain as an accompaniment. This is succeeded by a smaller cloud, and thus they continue, one succeeding the other, keeping you constantly on the lookout whilst on deck.

This afternoon the cry came again, 'Man overboard!' The ship was immediately hove to on the opposite tack, but fortunately for the man, as he could not swim, he had caught the stern drop-rope, and climbed up on deck without assistance. He fell from the fire-rigging and was more frightened than hurt. Lowered a boat and picked up our life-buoy, and filled away again.

During the evening we have had a fresh breeze and the horizon has been lined with squall, many of the heaviest of which we have avoided by going about. Still, every now and then we can hear them getting a wet jacket upon deck, but as the weather is so warm it don't [sic] matter much. We are now to the southward of the Bashee Group, the very nursery of typhoons, also of the Pratas Shoals. The next that we will encounter will be the Parac[el] and M[acclesfield] Shoals.

AUGUST 3RD

THURSDAY evening, 250 miles from Manila. Nothing can be more natural than the preference, at least aboard ship, of fair weather to foul for the purpose of writing. In fact, it is generally a matter of necessity as well as pleasure, it being next to an impossibility to hold securely and at the same time chair, book, and inkstand, and write withal. Such has been the case with myself for the last three or four days. The weather roll as the ship sinks into the yawning chasm formed by the receding sea; the deep lee[ward] lurch which buries her lee side, gun muzzles under, in the briny waves; the sudden shock of a heavy head sea which makes her tremble throughout her massive frame, as it strikes her bow with all its ponderous force, and sends its combing crest in upon the deck (much to the discomfiture of those ducked and consequent amusement of other who haply escape a wet jacket).

These and many other disadvantages that I might mention are incontrovertible difficulties both to penmanship and [to] that collected and undisturbed state of mind so necessary to the writer. And as I have said, such has been our situation for the last few days in quite an aggravated form. From whence it may readily be concluded that we have been experiencing heavy weather—and such has been the case; the weather becoming more and more stormy, the squalls heavier and in quicker succession, until at last it blew a gale accompanied by a heavy sea, both wind and sea being dead ahead. I feel assured that we have encountered, say, three squalls, that were as heavy as squalls could be, and we are very fortunate indeed in not having lost any of our important spars in them. In corroboration of which I will give a description of two, during the first of which I was officer of the deck. Some sea terms will be unavoidable, but I will make them as few as possible.

During the morning watch, the ship[having] been reefed down— that is, under easy sail—I had carried through several heavy squalls, one of which caught the sails aback, a thing to be dreaded. Fortunately, her headway was such as to enable her to pay off. At 8, orders came from the Captain to wear round. Hauled up the mainsail, and hauled down the spanker, then stationed the men for wearing.

Taking a look to windward to watch for a smooth chann[el], I noticed a tremendous squall coming down upon us. A deep, black, impenetrable mass extended along the horizon, and high above all rose a perfect black ring which gradually expanded until when overhead it broke. Then the squall struck us, accompanied by blinding sheets of rain which almost prevented our looking up. I had managed by this time to clew down the main and mizzen-topsails; not so the double-reefed fore-topsail and single-reefed foresail.

'Hard up the helm!'

But she would not go off, although no aftersail was set. Over on her lee side she lay at first, almost motionless; then gathering headway she sped like an arrow from the bow. Stronger and fiercer came the wind in overpowering force, until not only the fore-topmast, but the head of the foremast, bent like a wand—a thing I had never seen before. Attempted to take in the foresail, but tore it in doing so. Fortunately, the squall lasted but a few minutes, or we should have lost more of our sails.

In the afternoon I had just such another squall, though not so heavy. This time all sail was off the ship. Still later, towards evening, a threatening mass gathered on our weather quarter. We had wore[sic] round to avoid running into it, and the officer of the deck, supposing that it would pass astern, kept all sail on the ship; that is, close-reefed topsails and courses, which canvas, however, might be spread in an ordinary gale. Suddenly the squall changed its direction and came up to us right across the wind then blowing, and before we had time to let fly sheets and halliards, it struck us. The ship lay over motionless, the lee-quarter boat in the water, and green seas poured in our lee gun-deck ports, some of which were out for the sake of ventilation. Sheets and halliards were instantly let fly, for the ship was in danger. The main yard bowed up until we expected to hear it go with a crash every moment, but fortunately, it was cased in time. All hands, both officers and men, rushed on deck without being called, and by strenuous exertions we got all sail in safely, and the ship before the wind.

On examination, the main yard and heavy iron truss prove[d] both to have been very much strained, the latter having one of its iron bands moved out of place. Another such squall and the yard will certainly go. Should we lose it now with this head wind and sea, we would be obliged to bear up for some port to leeward.

FRIDAY MORNING, 4TH OF AUGUST, '54

HAVING written the above last night, I went on deck to assist in taking all sail off the ship. One of the most frightful looking squalls that could [be] imagined was coming up across the wind on our weather quarter. An immense black arc stretched across the heavens, rendered still blacker by the faint light of a quarter moon, whose dim rays shown forth through the flying scud; beneath this arc the sky had a livid hue, which shown like a brazen field when illumined by the glare of the lightning. The ocean looked as black as ink at first, till the force of the squall whitened its surface with sheets of foam. The whole aspect of sea and sky was truly grand, showing forth the power of the elements in all their majesty.

Today our canvas is spread to the breeze in wider folds, and the weather continues improving. We are still 200 miles from our port with a dead beat before us, but with ordinary weather we will soon accomplish it.

AUGUST 7TH, '54

16 days out from Keelung. Rain, rain, rain, day and night, and almost without intermission. This weather, we have every reason to suppose, will continue for the next month or two, it being the regular

rainy season. It does appear as if we were never to succeed in reaching our port, though distant only 90 miles. The blowy weather that we experienced so long still continues but with longer intervals between the squalls. Now, however, they often come up ahead or astern, the wind being very changeable. Still they do not blow fair for more than an hour or two in succession, invariably hauling again to the old quarter.

Most all of our sails have been split and torn, some two or three times, and a great many of the ropes have worn out and parted. Our bread will be out, as well as many other articles of provisions, in a few days, and it is full time for us to get in. Last night and, in fact, the day before, we got a distant glimpse of this land (the island, Lucon, or Luconia).[136] By making short tacks off and on we managed to keep within the influence of the land, ready to take advantage of the variables, but so far they have done us but little good. Our ship is wet fore and aft on all decks. Still, the weather being warm, the only inconvenience that we suffer from it, is that everything become moldy. All hands paddle about in their bare feet and southwesters (tarpaulin hats) and, smoking cheroots, take things quietly, on the principle that what cannot be cured must be endured.

AUGUST 9TH

OUR ship is now supposed to be in the latitude of Manila, perhaps to the southward of it. The exact position is not known, as we have not had a good observation for three or four days; and as we are continually changing our course and rate of sailing, but little confidence can be placed in the dead reckoning.

Yesterday we split the jib and two topgall[an]t sails, last night the mainsail and one topgall[an]t sail, and today have repaired the fore and mizzen-topsails, besides the jib twice. This morning I held on to the topg[allant] sails until our lee guns skimmed the water, ship going ten knots; five minutes after, and topsails were on the cap, and courses hauled up, to a very heavy squall. In the course of an hour, reefed and made sail again. This was hardly accomplished before all sail was taken in again to another heavy squall, after which double-reefed topsails and courses. In the afternoon clewed down again, which brings me up to the time of writing.

---

[136] Present Luzon, largest of the Philippine Islands.

At meridian ship was supposed to be 44 miles from Goat Island,[137] which is 30 miles from Manila, which bears from us, consequently, about S. E. by E.; distant some 40 miles. Could we feel assured that the above was actually the case we would keep away for our port, but should it be otherwise, and we should by so doing fall to leeward of the entrance to the harbour, we would be kept out two or three days longer, which is not to be desired at all. Tonight we will keep under short sail and tomorrow stand in with a fair wind, and, I hope, before night find ourselves safely at anchor in port. Though raining continually, and the ship, in consequence, never dry, still it is better weather for the men at least, than with a hot sun, light wind, and thermometer at 90 odd. In such weather the crew of a ship are always sickly from exposure, in[sufficient] use of water, and sleeping in heavy dews.

AUGUST 10TH

Tomorrow has come, and such a morrow as it had proved! This evening it blew a perfect hurricane and obliged us to furl every thing. A small tornado, if I may so call it, pass[ed] close to our bows, but fortunately cleared us. It raised a column of water on its course about twenty feet high and double that in diameter. If it had swept over us, one of our masts would have certainly gone.

During the night the weather has moderated. The morning finds us standing in towards the entrance of the extensive bay of Manila. As we enter the bay the wind and rain become more violent, the former shutting out the view entirely.

Meridian. It is now blowing a heavy gale, and with all sail furled, we are drifting in bodily towards our anchorage.

---

[137] Lubang Island.

At Anchor, Harbour
of
Manila

ONCE more we lay at rest, riding by our anchors, with no sail spread to the strong wind except our black storm awnings, which afford ample protection from the inclement weather. The weather lifting, so that we could see round us, we kept away, and without any sail came in at the rate of six or eight miles an hour and anchored something over two miles from the city, just outside the merchant shipping, of which there are a considerable number, [and] some of which I noticed by their colours to be Americans; and fine looking ships they are.

The boarding officer has been on board and speaks of the general health of the city being very good; not so of the weather, which he states to be very rainy. He inquired particularly if we expected any more of our squadron to visit the port, to which we gave an indefinite reply; that is, that they might or might not, such being the case.

The boarding boat was a very fine one, having quite a little house aft as a protection from the weather; pulled eighteen oars, with foresail and jib. Its whole appearance reminded me of the boats used for the same purposes in Rio de Janeiro.

We have boarded the American ships in port, of which there are four, two of them clippers: one, the *Winger* [sic] *Racer*[138] of New York; the other the *Seamen's Bride*[139] of Baltimore—the former 1700 tons and the latter 800.

The town or rather city of Manila is built at the head of the bay, forming a semicircle along the edge of the water. From a distance, the cathedral rises conspicuously above the evenly built town, which, though evidently extensive and covering a wide space of ground, yet

---

[138] The *Winged Racer* was built by Robert E. Jackson in East Boston in 1852.
[139] Built in 1851, the *Seamen's Bride* was considered a very fine example of Baltimore shipbuilding.

has a great sameness of appearance, all the buildings being of nearly an equal height.

Boarded an English ship[140] this morning that had made signal of distress (hoisting ensign Union down). Found the captain without a crew or officers, except a troublesome mate, who had attempted to rob him that night, and who[m] he was obliged to use force towards to retain him on board. As our ship lay near to his vessel, I told him we would keep a lookout whilst the matter was referred to the English Consul,[141] with which arrangement he rested satisfied. His little fat wife looked very much frightened, as it was in her division of the cabin the attempted robbery was made.

Two days' duty has passed, and now I am off for shore, and fun, too, if it can be had by perseverance. With a tin case packed, 48 hours' liberty before me, and a full purse. . . .! If time would permit, I would deliver some remarks appropriate to the occasion, but, all things considered, the following statement will suffice for the reflecting mind: 'Tin case, 48 h[ours'] liberty, full purse—O!' A melancholy fact which haply is not my present case. Eight months have we been away from civilized communities, the greater part of the time on salt provisions and bad flour. How pleasant must it be to us then to indulge in all the pleasures to be found in an enlightened port!

---

[140] The log of the *Macedonian* fails to mention this incident, and a careful search in the contemporary records proved to be unseccessful.

[141] John William Perry Farren was appointed Consul at Manila on May 30, 1844.

Visit
to Manila
Gala-Day

Left the ship early in the morning, in company with the doctor,[142] in one of the large passenger canoes of the country, the
only means of water conveyance that they have, with a top to protect
the occupant from the hot rays of the sun, and clean wooden seats.
They are by no means uncomfortable. Oars with broad, oblong
blades are used to propel them. Not a breath of air ruffled the water or
a cloud obscured the mid-summer sun, as we pushed off from the ship,
dressed in white and smoking our cheroots to beguile the time.

In the course of an hour we passed the lighthouse, entered the river,
or canal, as it is called, which divides the town in nearly two equal
portions, and, in keeping close to the breakwater side or right hand,
on which is considerable water battery, we proceeded up about a
quarter of a mile.

Crossed over, and, passing close to several large custom-house and
travelling boats with swivels mounted on their bows, stopped at the
landing near the hotel, the back entrance to which being closed,
walked round, [and], passing under a wide archway, we found ourselves in a spacious stone court, two sides of which were lined with
stables and carriage-houses, whilst a third gave admittance to the
hotel, which is situated on the 2d story, and, from its agreeable airy
construction, is worthy of a description.

The Fonda de Fernando is a large building, or rather, consisting
of two buildings connected by a third, which is principally a long
passage way lined with settees and shaded by veranda blinds on each
side. At one end is a billiard room; at the other, the office, which leads
into the *sall à manger*, a spacious dining-room, from whence you step
out upon a paved roof, as the Bunizarians call them. The bedrooms,

---

[124] Dr. Robert Woodworth.

which unfortunately are the least desirable feature of the hotel, are principally confined to the other buildings.

Having procured rooms and dressed for the day, we found on inquiry that our intended trip in the country, to breakfast with the Consul,[143] was not practicable, as our friend who was to have introduced us was then sitting quietly at the breakfast table. The hour for the morning meal in this country, being 10 a.m., had proved too much for his powers of endurance and he had succumbed, much to our disappointment; so we joined him there in discussing the contents of a well-spread board.

Breakfast over, the question was what should we do next. Too soon for visiting? Entirely. Too late for fashionable drives? Quite so. Then we will go [to] the cock-fights? The reply to the motion was unanimous, and ordering out the carriages we started for the cockpit.

Arriving at the enclosure, paid our two reals each, and, entering, passed up towards the place of combat, the whole way being lined with mestizos holding their game-cocks by a short string fastened round the leg. There were all colours and all sizes, many of them being fine specimens of their kind.

Entering a gateway and ascending by a bamboo ladder, we found ourselves in a moderate-sized box, evidently the best in the house. Beneath us was the cockpit, occupied by the judges, or, more properly, directors. It was a square piece of ground, surrounded by a fence, about the extent of a large room. On a level with our box extended a wide platform occupied by the betters, consisting of every caste and colour: priest and soldier, tradesman, merchant, and the native mestizo; all except the former dressed in gaudy-coloured garments, and everyone, without exception, smoking cheroots or cigarettes. A perfect Babel of tongues joined to laughter and wrangling, and the incessant crowing of cocks made the whole scene a quite exciting one.

Bets were made freely around us. A respectable-looking Spaniard sitting next to me pulled out a handful of doubloons from which to take his chance in the approaching combat. The most amusing sight, perhaps, of all was a young priest in his long serge gown and broad-brimmed hat, smoking a cigar at the same time as he passed round among the natives holding a box in his hand, one side of which was open for the reception of coins; and as he passed from one to the other

---

[143] William P. Pierce.

of the incongruous assembly, he held up the box for them to kiss, and then turned the open side towards [them] to receive the alms. I noticed, however, that he was not always successful, some only touching their caps when the box was presented, a sign of a polite refusal.

In the meantime bets were being made, averaging about $2 each, the highest a doubloon. Two or three pairs of cocks had been brought into the arena; but from some cause, either an unequal appearance or size, they were taken out again. At last, a fine pair came in, on which bets were freely offered; and as this is an amusement but little understood in our country, when conducted as it is here in its greatest perfection, I will describe one of the several fights that I wintessed so as to give a general idea of the proceedings. This being the favorite amusement of Manila, and on which considerable amounts of money change hands every day, some follow it no doubt as a living.

Two fine cocks were brought in, so equally matched that it was difficult to say which would come off victorious. One was red and the other a clear golden colour. The eyes of both were fierce and bloodshot, and as their keepers advanced them towards each other they struggled hard to come together. At last, a sufficient number of bets being made, the keepers screwed on the long steel gaffs, which were as sharp as razors, both on point and edge. This being completed, each was allowed to peck the head of the other twice, which had certainly the same effect as might be expected from one pugilistic character striking another; for the moment they were placed opposite to each other, and the signal given, they flew at each other with great impetuosity, both falling heavily to the ground with the force of the shock. Again they faced each other, and made two or three feints, to gain advantage of position; and once more they closed and fell. The red cock rose quickly; the other more slowly as if he could hardly stand, still showing, however, a bold front. But he had alreay received his death wound, the gaff of his opponent having pierced its full length into his breast. His strength was gone, and, unable to meet the last and fatal shock of his victorious enemy, fell dead at his conqueror's feet. The building resounded with acclamations as the victor stood with raised head and expanded front in the midst of the arena, with his vanquished enemy at his feet, truly monarch of all he surveyed.

Sometimes a wing is cut off, and again a head, shunning the force of the blow and the sharpness of the instrument which produces the fatal effect.

From the cockpit we drove round to the American Consul's residence, a large spacious buiding with office in the front part and storehouse in the rear, facing the canal, as do all business houses, the second story being appropriated to the uses of the family. This we reached by a circular broad flight of stairs, of easy ascent, and were ushered into a parlor, which for size and arrangement surpassed anything I had as yet seen on the station. Fine prints and engravings ornamented the rose-coloured walls, and the floor of dark grained wood was polished to perfect smoothness, each plank being near a foot in width. The walnut and cane furniture were of ample dimensions and tastefully distributed about the apartment. At one end stood handsomely carved bookcase, filled with neatly bound standard and light works. At the opposite extremity was placed a large piano and music stand; in the several recesses were oblong or square tables of the various woods of the country; and in the centre stood a large round Chinese table with marble top which in make (not size) reminded me very much of the one at home.

The Consul not being in, we sat down and passed an hour or so agreeably reading the papers, both of home and abroad. And so the old church of St. Paul's[144] has been burned down—buried with its past memories of pleasant times! Years bring their changes, scarcely perceptible to those who witness them from day to day, as in the natural course of events their cycles are completed, but strongly impressed upon the mind when the various changes which occur during their slow but unerring round become known collectively, not singly. How many of us now say daily, 'Two-thirds or more of a year have passed since home news has been received.' How I long to receive confirmation of hopes and happiness, and yet, how I fear! May we, like the pilot, fear not, but trust in Providence wherever we may be. A week more and, when passed, may we all rejoice. Bow, ye favouring winds, speed our gallant bark on her watery way! But to return to Manila:

We were reading in the Consul's parlor, and he in the country. Leaving our cards, prepared to depart, when we encountered our old shipmates, the Salababoos[145] [sic], residing here temporarily. If

---

[144] St. Paul's Protestant Episcopal Church in Baltimore. 'On Saturday morning, April 29, 1854, shortly after one o'clock, the stately edifice was discovered to be in flames. . . . The firemen labored hard to arrest the progress of the flames, but this was impossible in consequence of the elevated position of the building and the scarcity of water.' HISTORY OF BALTIMORE CITY AND COUNTY, by John Thomas Scharf. pp. 520-521.

[145] 'On the morning of the 5th of August, 1853, in about latitude 18° 46' N., longitude 124° E., the store-ship *Southampton*, Lieutenant Commander Boyle, was steering with considerable swell, when a boat was discovered to windward. The ship was hove to, and pre-*

these people ever again reach their native land, what wonders will they tell of fine ships and foreign lands! But I much doubt if they ever will see their own country again. Living aboard of our ships as they have for the last years, they show great disinclination to being left on shore in charge of[the] Goverment, but such is their fate.

From the Consul's, returned to the hotel or Fonda, and seated ourselves to tiffin, after which enjoyed a siesta and a cigar. In the early part of the afternoon, Mr. Green, an extremely obliging gentleman of the firm of [Russell, Sturgis and Co.][146] called in to pay a visit to the officers. After an hour's agreeable conversation, he invited us to dine with him at five, which we politely accepted; and drove round at the appointed time to the large and ample residence of the firm. I have always noticed that those who live abroad in foreign countries always compensate, to the best of their ability, for the loss of home and its associations, by a profuse manner of living, combining the more practical methods of prosecuting business with the enjoyment of that ease and luxury so well understood and systematically carried in tropical countries.

This firm in particular had existed for years in a flourishing condition, the original members being long since dead. The building in size and internal arrangement resembles much the residence of the Consul, on a larger scale. From the balcony of the drawing-room you have a fine view of the principal cathedral, a large weather-beaten building surmounted by a dome and cross, being situated on ground considerably elevated above the common level. The prospect of the country round must be very fine from its summit.

In the course of a few minutes, the gentlemen of the establishment commenced dropping in one by one, until our number increased to a dozen or more. Having gone through the form of introduction, the conversation became general and various interesting subjects of

---

*sently succeeded in getting on board the boat and its contents. . . . On board of the boat, were six males, four of whom were adults and two were boys. . . . To what nation or people these poor creatures belonged no one could tell, as no body on board could understand their language. It was observed, however, that the word most frequently on their lips was *Sil-li-ba-boo*. . . . One purpose of the visit of the *Macedonian* to Manila was to hand them over to the governor general of the Philippines.' THE EXPEDITION OF AN AMERICAN SQUADRON. v. 1. pp. 501-504.

146 In the early part of the 19th century, there were two American firms in Manila: Russel, Sturgis and Co., and Peel, Hubbell and Co. The former was founded by J. and T.H. Perkins of Canton, China, and their Manila branch was managed by Jonathan and George R. Russel, and one Sturgis. They advertised their firm by lavish entertainment, giving big dinners and receptions almost nightly and kept practically open house in Manila. *See:* Antonio M. Regidor y Jurado and J. Warren T. Mason. COMMERCIAL PROGRESS IN THE PHILIPPINE ISLANDS London, 1905.

discourse were introduced. Of Japan they knew much more than we expected, which information they had gained from the Russian Admiral,[147] who had resided with them during his stay at Manila (of which fact I noticed they were rather proud).

They gave us the first reliable information that we had received of the reception of the Russian fleet at Nagasaki.[148] It appears the representative of the Autocrat had received many presents (principally of soi[149] [sic] and raw silks) from that Japanese, but as to the treaty he had been entirely unsuccessful, and that the Russian Admiral had expressed it as his opinion that no nation would ever succeed in establishing a friendly intercourse with that people, which statement we have disproved. Among the gentlemen present was Mr. Munford[150] [sic], brother to the gentleman of that name not long since murdered in his office at the Manila rope works, of which he was proprietor, and as an enquiry into the true causes of that cold-blooded assassination was one reason of our visiting the port, I will here give a short statement of the case.

Mr. Munford[151] was an American, and considerably advanced in age. He was generous and kind, and well-beloved by the mestizos, or natives, who[m] he employed, as well as by others with whom in a business way he had no connection. It appears that the last pay-day of the workmen, the amount being unusually large, they were obliged to postpone the payments of a portion for two or three days. This was Saturday. On the following morning, whilst sitting in his office in company with a merchant family,[152] some thirty disguised natives entered, and killed them both, making their escape in safety, nor have any since been apprehended by the authorities. Mr. Munford received

[147] Evfimii Vasil'evich Putiatin Vice admiral and count, and commander of the Russian fleet to Japan between 1852–54.

[148] On August 21, 1853, four Russian warships entered Nagasaki harbor with a suggestion for the delimitation of the Russian and Japanese territories in the Northern Seas and a request that Japan should open one or two ports to Russian vessels and trade. After several meetings between the commissioners of the Shogunate and Putiatin, the delimitation problem had to be left unsettled. As to the opening of a port near Yedo and another in the north, Russia was to be placed on the same footing as other foreign nations. When he left Nagasaki on February 5, 1854, Putiatin failed to obtain any material advantage.

[149] Soy beans

[150] Charles D. Mugford.

[151] Brother of Charles D. Mugford was killed in March, 1853, by several Spaniards at a rope factory at Santa Mesa, within the jurisdiction of the governor of the Philippines. To Captain Abbot's inquiry, replies Marquse de Novaleches, Governor of the Islands: '. . . . Since the day in which this very sad affair took place, the courts have not ceased in their investigation and inquiries. . . . These courts have established and judged the case. They will continue to fulfil their mission for the punishment of the two presumed criminals, the only ones which they have not been able to find, but who will suffer the penalty they merit if they are still in the islands and have not escaped abroad.' THE EXPEDITION OF AN AMERICAN SQUADRON. v. 2, p. 147.

[152] The search failed to disclose the name of the second man murdered at this time.

upwards of thiry mortal wounds on his person. Such are all the facts known of the case.

Dinner being announced, we adjourned to the dining saloon. Of the several *recherché* courses politeness forbids me to speak. The same may be said of the tasteful display of china and silver service. The refreshing breezes of the gently swinging punka added considerably to the enjoyment of the repast.

An evidently well-informed person who sat opposite to me mentioned several facts of interest in respect to the country and its inhabitants, many of which I regret having forgotten. He mentioned one singular circumstance, however, which is well worth noting; namely, that all the provinces, towns, streets, roads, and many public works were named after the vegetable kindgom of the Island. The word 'Manila' itself being the name of a tree, once common, but now extinct in the Island.

It appears from this gentleman's account, that there has been recently signs of a rising in the Island to overthrow the present government, which did not take place, however, in consequence of the want of energy or courage on the part of subordinates concerned therein. Government becoming cognizant of the fact, and fearing, not without cause, the result, issued an order, which they have since enforced with unremitted vigor, that no foreigner, resident or transient, should visit the provinces, or proceed more than seven miles in any direction beyond the precincts of the city,[153] and that every native, to gain access from one to any other portion of the country, should be required to furnish himself with a passport. This restriction under existing circumstances is certainly very justifiable in the authorities; but that which caused the necessity of the act, was brought about by various former arbitrary measures, enforced to the evident injury of the mass of the inhabitants, and, complaint being useless, the desire of revolting became general. But to continue my personal movements: having dined, returned to the drawing-room, lighted cheroots, and partook of a cup of coffee, *à la turk*, then of a thimbleful of maraschino.

The sun was now nearly set, and this being the fashionable time to take an airing, a gentleman, by name Mr. Lorry, politely invited me to accompany him in his carriage, and allow him to act as my *cicerone*, which request I gladly accepted, and together we set out for a pleasant drive on the Cassadra.

---

[153] By Royal Ordinance of 1844, strangers were excluded from the interior.

G

I must deviate here a moment to give expression to my thoughts, they being also my opinion and feelings at the time. Spanish society and Spanish custom, alike, have in all cases, I may say, shown a happy forbearance in drawing the line of demarkation between the refined usages of life and the personal comforts of the individual, showing practically the possibility of the two being so combined that, without infringement upon either, the one may be practiced, at the same time that the other is enjoyed—a method of combination and a height of refinement equalled only by the French, and not always by them, their volatility of character often rendering the attempt ridiculous. In fact, every nation has its characteristics. That which is *comme il faut* in one is *parvenu* in another. What would be thought of two persons in white jackets and straw hats, smoking cigars, and driving through Hyde Park, London? The very least that would be done would be to turn them out, yet during this pleasant evening's drive, such was our costume, and our occupation the same. Nor was it considered, in the least, a deviation from strict propriety.

Of the various costumes, both of town and peasantry that I have seen in various parts of the world, I think perhaps none are more truly picturesque than the varied-coloured habiliments of the Manilanese women. Red, yellow, and green skirts and handkerchiefs, with the parti-coloured mestizo slipper peeping out, formed a brilliant contrast with the dusky complexion and coal-black hair of the wearers. As we rumbled over the bridge and passed under the arched gateway which gives admittance within the walled portion of the town, it appeared as if we had entered a new city, so different was the whole scene from that we had just left.

Without the walls, though the large cathedral, several smaller ones, handsome foreign residences, besides rows of well-furnished stores tend much to beautify that portion of the town, still the greater portion is composed of muddy streets lined with two-story bamboo houses with rush tops, which have a very disfiguring effect.

Within, all is different. The silent, clean, and well-paved streets, the high yellow-coloured houses with their white cornices and jalousied windows, all speak the Spanish town. The convent, the church, the place, the prison, and, lastly, the plaza but confirm the impression. Yes, this is Manila proper. Here no foreigners can reside; although otherwise they have free access within its precincts when they please.

Continuing on our way, we passed out beyond the walls and in a few minutes were in the vortex of carriages and horses which crowded the Cassadra. Very refreshing was the breeze that came from the rippling waters of the harbour, and still more pleasant was the sound of a fine brass band, performing a piece from Lucretia Borgia, in which the full, round, mellow notes of the trombone, exquisitely played, rose high above the other instruments. Stopped our carriage to enjoy the scene and music. There was the Governor[154] in his carriage and four (and he alone can drive that number).

Here and there and everywhere round were liveried carriages occupied by ladies, two in each, and other of the merchants and Spanish gentlemen. The gallant portion of the male community passed their time walking from one carriage to the other, conversing with or simply saluting their fair occupants. My friend was evidently of a rather phlegmatic disposition and not to be caught by straws, for although his polite bow of recognition showed that he knew almost every lady present; yet in a few minutes, the music being finished for the evening, we drove off and continued our drive into the country, which was very pretty, and did not reach the city again until it was dark. Drove to the hotel and refreshed ourselves with, among other nice things, an American ham, which to us was quite a delicacy.

Having rested sufficiently, we drove round to the theater, which is now where the Melodeon or music hall was formerly, the theater proper having fallen in some time previous. The audience was small in number but select in appearance, the actors and actresses passable, and the play the same no doubt—at least in subject—as may be seen or heard in St. Petersburg at this time; namely, love and the obstacles attending its happy consummation. The female portion of the spectators did not overcome me with their glances, perhaps because they never glanced at me.

However, taking advantage of the first pause in the performance, we returned to our carriage and drove round to the plaza, and stopping near the church of St. Domingo, listened to the performance of three brass bands combined, which, in the still night (and the moon shown brightly) was delicious. From our position we looked upon the Governor's palace, the prison of state opposite, diplomacy buildings, and the cathedral mentioned before. Gradually the bands filed off one by one, and the square became deserted.

Directing the driver to convey us to the Fonda, I there bid my

---

[154] El Marques de Novaleches.

friend *bueno nos noche* [*sic*] and retired to my room, not to sleep, but to meditate on the various little amusement[s] of the day, which I had enjoyed the more from my long abstinence from all such pleasures. At about midnight turned in for a nap, but it [was] impossible to sleep, my room being immediately over one of the stables, in which the horses were making all im[aginable] noise[s], which were so unfamiliar to me that after tossing about the bed for an hour or more, I was obliged at last to turn out and go down, where having identified two or three of the most unruly, I had them removed, no doubt much to their discomfort. The remainder of the night was passed in oblivion.

In the morning, having employed the services of a Spanish barber, and thereby learned more fully to appreciate Murray,[155] I dressed and in company with the doctor (Woodworth, an intimate friend of Nicholson's)[156] took a pleasant drive through the town and returned in time for breakfast. It now commenced rain, much to our disappointment. This did not deter me, however, from making my purchases, which, being principally for others, and Watters in particular (the most difficult man in the squadron to please), was a source of much gratification to me when completed.

A French dentist had called in the morning whilst I was engaged fitting eighteen buttons into as many small holes in a jacket, which, having already occupied more than half an hour, had considerably ruffled my temper (inwardly) so that my French was not very fluent when I joined him and undertook to explain my wants. This by no means restored my equanimity, for the last words that the *maitre d'hotel* had said to him, after introducing us, was, 'He will understand you.'' Nevertheless, I had my teeth put in order and saved two thereby. Folks at home with dentists all round them do not know their value until they are situated like ourselves; that is, only one dentist on the station, and the port where he resides accidentally visited.

This accomplished and the weather clearing up, the first lieutenant[157] and myself drove round to a French variety store, where between the politeness of monsieur and the flattery of madame at my perfect pronunciations I spent treble the am[ount] I intended and came [a]way highly satisfied with myself.

Passengers by the Spanish steamer had arrived at the Fonda during our absence, amongst whom were two rather handsome girls, and

[155] Probably the name of a barber on the *Macedonian*.
[156] Lieutenant James William Augustus Nicholson (1821–87) of the *Vandalia*.
[157] Kidder Randolph Breese.

they were to appear at dinner. Caught a glimpse of them and felt so well satisfied that I immediately put on my best bib and tucker for the occasion. In due time the company assembled at the dinner table, and I discovered to my great disappointment that my reserved seat, next to Breese by agreement, was on the same side and much lower down than those of the Spanish ladies, who were being entertained by a number of gentlemen countrymen of theirs, a gray-mustached Spanish colonel among the number.

An explanation ensued. 'He is the husband of one, and the other is married also,' said my informant, Breese. I was satisfied, and went through the regular courses, concluding with coffee and cigar, with undiminished gusto.

The present frequenters of the hotel are, I imagine, composed of the same classes of society as may be found there at any time of the year, such as Spanish army officers, not on present duty; merchant captains, English and American principally; a few of the more wealthy storekeepers of the town (Monsieur Dupuis among the number); transient travellers; and officers belonging to the men-of-war in port. Of the former class there was one, a Colonel Delamiers, *aide-de-camp* to the former governor, a tall fine-looking man with gray mustache, Irish by birth, and consequently a soldier of fortune. He was the only man I ever saw in my life who bore any resemblance to General Washington. Of the merchant captains little need be said. Those of our own country were by far superior to the rest. Strength of language and impetuosity of manner were common to all alike.

Another evening, and of course another drive, and, as I expected, a pleasant one. Breese and myself in a carriage together pioneered by an advance vehicle containing two Spanish chief engineers (Englishmen); one of whom having lately arrived from Southampton, we had many agreeable reminiscences to recall and friends to enquire of, and were happy to find that all remained in *statu quo*[sic]. It being rather early, we first drove through the city, crossing the wire suspension bridge, which is, I should say, three or four hundred feet in length, spanning the river, on the banks of which were a great number of canoes loading with cut grass, some of them full seventy feet in length, and formed from a single tree. The bridge was constructed in England, by order.

On our first arrival we were told to expect nothing but rain during our stay. Such fortunately was not the case, otherwise many of my little personal adventures would never have been written. The afternoon of this day had been clear, the atmosphere cooled by the morning's shower, and the bright drops still sparkled on the foliage of the country. We were passing by an avenue of trees, beneath which were gathered men and women, boys and girls, laughing and chatting and enjoying themselves with that pleasing exuberance of spirits so consonant with the place and the hour.

Suddenly the deep-toned notes of the cathedral bell came booming through the air with slow and measured beat, telling that the setting sun was low. Hushed was the voice of mirth, uncovered was every head, and silently the evening prayer ascended to Him above. The bell ceased, and all was life and gaiety again. The effect produced upon the mind by this act of devotion, in which unison of purpose pervades the hearts of a great community at one time, is very beneficial; and it is to [be] hoped that custom does not lessen the effect.

This evening we continued our ride long after dark. At one moment we were passing the margin of a small stream, and then the view would be shut out by the thick shrubbery round us. Returning to the city we passed the Hall of Justice brilliantly illuminated. At first we thought it was the opening of a ball and consequently ordered the carriage to stop. The driver undeceiving us, continued on our way. Caught a fleeting glimpse of a carriage occupied by an interesting couple, the gentleman having his arm affectionately passed round the waist of his fair partner (to be for life, I suppose), those being the symptoms to entering the traces (to be reined in with a curb bit).

Stopped at a small though well-furnished café where lemonade and soda were being dispensed to a select few. Indulged in the refreshing beverage ourselves, and having smoked and chatted awhile returned to the Fonda. A cup of coffee and to bed. Up early next morning. Packed up and in company with Lieuten[an]t Breese pushed off for the ship in a canoe, well satisfied with my two days' visit to the city of Manila and hoping that it would not prove my last opportunity of enjoyment in this prince of places on the East India Station, Japan included.

On my return on board, found the ship in excellent order; the paint work touched up, the decks thoroughly cleaned, the yards square, sails snugly furled, and rigging taut. The crew also were dressed in muster clothes. This, in connection with the bustle and activity displayed by everyone, convinced me that something unusual was about to occur. On inquiry such proved to be the case. The Military Governor and staff, merchants of Manila, and several clipper captains were to visit the ship that day by invitation from the Captain.

In due time, our boats were sent to the landing in charge of officers to convey them on board. The Military Governor is the second in command (the Governor himself, being in mourning at present, did not attend). Saluted his representative on his arrival aboard, and having beat to quarters they went the rounds of the ship, and expressed satisfaction at everything they saw. We also fired several shell guns at their request, and it mortifies me to say that our shell have become injured by various exposures, so that about only every other one will burst. The retreat having been beaten, all hands adjourned to the cabin and ward rooms, where they were entertained quite handsomely, and concluded the morning's variety by smoking Japanese pipes and examining the various curiosities brought from that country by our officers.

I presented the genlemen to whom I was indebted for the agreeable evening's ride, with a Japanese pipe, some tobacco, and a *Sakê* cup, which favour he returned on the following day with a box of *Regalias*, a cigar, at present just introduced here and consequently very fashionable and difficult to obtain.

On leaving, saluted the American Consul with nine guns, the American ensign at the fore. The men having behaved very well today whenever their services were required, the Captain, as an indulgence, spliced the main brace.*

*"spliced the main brace" means the captain gave the men an extra allowance of spirits.

The American Ships
At Anchor in
the Harbour of Manila

IN no part of the world do you see as many fine specimens of marine architecture as in the East Indies. The general character of the winds in these seas require[s] vessels of sharp mold to be employed in the trade. This fact was so well understood years ago by those concerned in the Chinese commerce, that clippers were long used for such voyages before they were known in other countries. Now they are the popular ships of the day, and I feel convinced that in less than a dozen years full-built ships will have disappeared from off the ocean. The Americans excel without a doubt all other nations in shipbuilding, and will, I hope, continue to do so. At present there are five American merchant ships in the harbor, the largest being the clipper ship *Winged Racer* (1700 tons measurement). She is a very fine-looking vessel, long black hull and tapering spars. The next in consequence is the Baltimore clipper, *Seamen's Bride* (750 tons), a vessel well-known by her quick passages on several occasions,[158] and which I last saw some three years ago, lying alongside the w[h]arf, loading for her first voyage. Besides these, there are two Boston ships of 6 or 7 hundred tons burthen,[159] the names of which I do not know, and lastly, the brig *Brenda*[160] (250 tons, carrying four brass twelves). Last year we passed her at sea, rigged as a schooner. She is now a brig bound to St. [sic] Francisco. She belongs to the opium trade, in which she has been very successful. I was officer of the deck when she came in (12 days from Hongkong) and thought her a

---

[158] The *Seamen's Bride* and *Winged Racer* sailed from New York and Boston on 23rd and 24th of January, 1854, respectively, both arriving San Francisco on May 23rd, the race going to the *Winged Racer* by a margin one day over the *Seamen's Bride*.

[159] As far as I could determine, the *Fearless* of Boston, built in 1853, and commanded by Nehimiah Manson, and the *John Bertram* also

of Boston, built in 1845, and commanded by Frederick Lendholm, are the only American clippers that were in Manila harbor in the latter half of 1854.

[160] The last of the American opium clippers *Brenda* was a 300 ton schooner, built by George Raynes of Portsmouth, New Hampshire, in 1851.

man-of-war brig—although she showed no pennant—on account of her square sails, guns, and general appearances. She is one of six pioneer clippers modelled by Captain Goldsborough[161] of the Navy, present superintendent at the Naval Academy.

Tobacco, sugar, rice, and hemp (or Manila grass) are the principal exports of the Island.

Fresh provisions are obtained here in abundance. Of the fruits, the mango is by far the superior. They are about six inches in length and four in width, of an oblong form and nearly round. Opened with a silver knife and eaten with a spoon, the soft, rich, yellow fruit dissolves in your mouth like ice-cream. I have eaten them in Brazil, China, and Formosa; but this is entirely a different fruit, and I have no doubt the reason that more mention has not been made of it is that men-of-war very rarely visit this port in the summer season, and it is only then that they can be procured in any degree of perfection.

Breese is endeavouring to take two hundred of them to China as a present to a lady friend. The first four days (we are now out six) not one of them showed signs of over-ripening, but since then we have been obliged to consume eight or ten of them daily to prevent their spoiling, no very difficult duty to perform as you may well imagine. We expect tomorrow a rich harvest, as a dozen or more appear nearly ready for consumption. It is to be hoped for the sake of the lady that our ship will reach her port the day after, otherwise her portion will be small, as the doctor has recommended them to us as a diet, and I notice that Breese, in making his decision, required the existence of very few specks to condemn the one in question, in spite of his good intentions.

---

[161] Louis Malesherbes Goldsborough (1805–77), was superintendent of the Naval Academy from 1853–57.

Manila Cigars

IT is but due to the place (and my own inclination) that at least a few lines should be dedicated to this subject. Chewing tobacco is a peculiarity of our own country and sea-faring persons of all nations. Smoking is a world-wide custom, confined to no particular grade or even sex. The Indians' calumet was emblematic of peace, the hooka of Indies denotes the hour of relaxation, the nargileh of the Turk is the mark of friendship, and the meerschaum of the Dutchman is his silent companion in the moments of reverie. The opium pipe of the Chinaman declares the infatuation of his race. The American's cigar proves the excitement necessary to his nature; that of the Spaniard's the love of ease and quiet enjoyment. High and low, rich and poor, alike, indulge to excess in the use of the narcotic weed, but without any injurious effects from the indulgence. The secret of the matter is easily explained: they are a temperate race, coffee and light wines being the extent of their libations.

All the luxuries of life cannot be indulged in with impunity by the same person. Men are not all constituted alike. That which affords pleasure without injury to one, may be prejudicial to another. This is applicable to the uses of tobacco, [wines], and what is generally called 'high living'. Their use is a pleasure; their abuse a vice. The commingling of all insures the loss of health. The first *ad libitum*, the last in moderation, fulfil the extent of my personal desires.

As I have previously remarked, every nation uses tobacco with a different intent; and the effect produced supports the supposition. The Dutchman is most thoughtful under the soothing influence of his meerschaum, the latent faculties of the Chinaman are aroused by the exciting effects of his opium pipe; the irritable temperament of the Saxon becomes relaxed for the moment, and whilst in the enjoyment of his cigar, wishes it was always after dinner in this world. For my own part, I always have remarked and noticed, that, with very few exceptions, persons who are regular and constant smokers, and at the same time temperate and moderate in their habits, take more pleasure in the quiet enjoyments of home, and are apt to be of a thoughtful turn of mind (two desiderata which require, however, time and means).

As to the tobacco of Luçon (Luconia). The tobacco of the Islands is mild, of a light colour, and easily worked. Of good quality, though not what is styled rich flavoured, age much improves it. Before visiting the port, I supposed that there were but two forms or rather two kinds of cigars manufactured; namely, the cheroot No. 1 (large size), No. 2 (medium size), and the Havana shaped cigar, No. 2 size. But on the contrary, the varieties are numbers. Commencing with cheroots, of this form there are Nos. 1, 2, 3. The No. 1's are of such a size that you are obliged to put the smaller or wrong end in the mouth. No. 2 is the size exported and for sale in the cigar stores at home. No. 3 is more commonly used by the mestizo women, who are constant smokers. Of cigars, there are four sizes, Nos. 1, 2, and 3 corresponding with the cheroots of similar numbers. The smaller variety of this form (No. 4) are [sic] filled with fine tobacco, the same as cigarettes, which they have also. In our country, cigars of this size are designated ladies' cigars.

Besides these several varieties, there is another, of which I have a few as a sample, which is not only never exported, but which several of the first merchants said they had never seen before. These cigars are styled *cavillieros*, and made of the choicest tobacco in the most careful manner. In length they are about seven inches, I should think, and smoke pleasantly. The Governor presented the Captain with 4000 of them, some of which he very kindly presented to the officers. The *Regalia* (No. 1 Havana shape) have also but lately been introduced. The tobacco being the very best and the number of boxes for sale few, causes a great rush when they are disposed of at auction, so that those who obtain them consider themselves fortunate. I am indebted to a friend for the presentation of a box.

Relative prices of cheroots:

Cheroots				*Cigars*		
No. 1. $14 per 1000				No. 1. $22 per 1000		
" 2. $ 8 " "				" 2. $ 8 " "		
" 3. $ 7 " "				" 3. $ 7 " "		
				" 4. $ 6 " "		

The above prices are, I think, exact.

Cheroots are put up in boxes of 500 each, except No. 1, which, like the *Regalia* (No. 1 cigar shape), are in boxes holding 125 each. Cigars were at one time exported in large numbers, to prevent which their manufacture was forbidden. I think, however, Mr. Groswell proposed to the Governor a method of remedying what they called an evil by making them up in paper packages containing 125 or 150 in each. This was adopted, and now the regulation is that only one or two packages can be purchased, by the person sent, at a time; and the merchant captains say that they are obliged to pay duty even on one package when they take it off to the ship for immediate use.

Cheroots were formely sold at a reduced price, the purchasers afterwards speculating upon them in Australia and California trade, which, by the by, in connection with the regular trade carries them off as fast as they can be manufactured, so that an old cigar cannot be procured. Government being desirous of making all the profit themselves have now adopted the plan of a duo-weekly sale by auction at slightly advanced prices and a rigid prohibition for purchasers to sell them again at advanced rates. This last clause refers to all kind[s] of manufactured tobacco.

Cheroots are styled—— (——) from the peculiar manner of making them; cigars [cavillieros] (——) to distinguish them from the cheroot.

Regalias are named from their counterparts in Havana, they being imitations of the cigar of that name manufactured in Cuba, which being the case, I will now go and smoke one (10 o'clock at night), in conformance with our established custom at home, much to the evident satisfaction of (all hands), mother included.

APPENDIX

§1. LETTERS, EAST INDIA SQUADRON,
1854–56

No. 3

U. S. SHIP *Macedonian*
CANTON RIVER, WHAMPOA, CHINA
OCTOBER 7TH, 1854

Sir:

......I have deemed it necessary and proper to appoint, which I did on the 25th ultimo, Passed Midshipman John G. Sproston as Acting Master of the U. S. Chartered Steamer Queen, *and also to do the duty, when circumstances will allow, of Flag Officer of the Squadron, which appointment I respectfully request you may be pleased to approve and to sanction his continuing an Acting Master in the performance of the duties of Flag Officer after the necessity of his services in the* Queen *shall cease. A Flag Officer may be termed 'Captain of the Fleet' or 'Flag Lieutenant' or 'Flag Officer', according to rank and circumstances, which is simply an Officer acting as confidential aid to a Commander of a Fleet or Squadron. Such an aid I desire, and Mr. Sproston, with the rank of Acting Master, will be adequate to meet my wants and wishes......*

Very respectfully Sir
I have the honor to be
Your Obt. Servant
(signed) JOEL ABBOTT
Captain U. S. Navy
Senior Officer Comd. U. S. Squadron
East India and China Seas

I. C. DOBBIN
SECRETARY OF THE NAVY,
WASHINGTON CITY, D. C.,
U.S. AMERICA

H

§2. LETTERS, EAST INDIA SQUADRON,
1854–56

No. 16
U. S. FLAG SHIP *Macedonian*
HONG KONG, APRIL 4TH, 1855

Sir:

......*I also acknowledge the receipt of your letter of January 9th, 1855,
and beg leave to remark upon its contents respecting the appointments con-
ferred upon Passed Midshipmen John Watters and John G. Sproston as
Acting Masters, the Department saying 'it cannot as at present advised,
approve, as there would be Passed Midshipmen senior to them in the Squadron
to which they are attached, acting in inferior stations'. Such is not the case.
There is not a Passed (or any other) Midshipman acting as such in the
Squadron. Mr. Watters was made Acting Master of the Macedonian by
Commodore Perry on the 29th of August 1854, just before the sailing of the
return ships; but before making the appointment he sent for all the Passed
Midshipmen belonging to the vessels about to return to the U. States, and
offered to each, beginning with the Senior the appointment of Acting Master
of the Macedonian, but they all preferred rather to return home than to stop
out and be promoted; so Mr. Watters received the appointment.*

*When I made Mr. Sproston Acting Master of the Chartered Steamer
Queen, and to be my flag officer when not serving on board of her, he was
the only Passed Midshipman in the Squadron acting as such. The reduction
of officers in the Squadron has since made it necessary to place Mr. Sproston
as Acting Master of the* Macedonian *and to let Mr. Watters do the duty of
Lieutenant with the rank of Acting Master only. These explanations I trust
will be satisfactory and that you will be pleased to allow these two worthy
officers to receive the rank and pay of Acting Master......*

*I have the honor to be,
Very respectfully
Your obedient Servant,*

MR. I. C. DOBBIN

SECRETARY OF THE NAVY,

WASHINGTON CITY, D.C.,

U.S. AMERICA.

(signed) JOEL ABBOTT
*Commanding U. S. Squadron
East India and China Seas*

§3. LETTERS, EAST INDIA SQUADRON,
1854–56

U.S. STEAMER *Queen*
AT ANCHOR OFF THE ISLAND OF TOKYO
NOV. 13, 1854

Sir:

In obedience to your orders, and at the commencement of the action on the morning of the 13th inst. shoved off from the Queen *in the* Macedonian's *armed Pinnace, having besides the crew of the boat the following American Gentlemen as volunteers, namely, General James Keenan, Am. Consul at Hong Kong and Messrs. L. Moses of Macao, and F. W. Alford of Canton. Immediately on leaving the steamer found the boat within range of the Pirates battery on shore, several of the shot passing close to the boat, and one striking the after oar on the off side. Knowing that our small boat gun would be useless at that distance I did not stop to fire, but pulled across the harbor to join the English forces, their boats having taken position close in to the shore on the port hand. Finding the landing party disembarking, immediately did the same under cover of the spirited fire from the Portuguese Government Lorcha, three steamers and English gunboats. The Pirates directed several of their guns so as to bear upon us, but without doing any injury. Having landed, formed my men in single file, and proceeded with all the celerity the nature of the ground would admit of, following a party of Marines who had landed from the first boat. As we neared the battery noticed the Pirates deserting their guns in great numbers and by the time our joint forces had reached the head of the bay and formed into platoons they were in full flight. As yet we had fired only irregular shots from our small arms, having met with no combined resistance from the Pirates. Our order of battle being formed, Marines on the right hand and sailors on the left, the whole under command of Lieut. Fellowes, R. N., took up our line march towards the opposite end of the valley, the main body passing close to a long line of junks moored head and stern in a shallow stream. In the meantime the American gentlemen, mentioned before acting separately from the regular force, had pursued their course along the beach, pulling down the Enemies' flags as they reached them, and as I have been since informed assisted in securing a number of prisoners from on board the Junks. We had not proceeded far before our line became very much broken by the narrow paths we were obliged to follow, order was again restored, and the word passed to cease firing, as no Pirates appeared on the decks of the Junks. It was about this time that a gentleman, the Am. Consul as I have since learned, was noticed to be in great danger, he being exposed to the fire of*

*a fort, they at the same time attempting to surround him. There was an
instantaneous rush on the part of the Landing Force which created considerable
confusion in the ranks, the commanding officer attempted to reform them, which
caused a momentary pause, but the nature of the ground was such as to prevent
any regularity of attack, and the word was given to forward, which we did,
pouring in a volley when within half musket range. This had the desired effect,
the Pirates deserted their guns, and the flag of the fort was hauled down by
the Am. Consul. The Commanding Officer of the division, noticing the flight
of the Pirates, ordered the Marines to advance to the front, and the Blue
Jackets to ascend the hills which were close at hand, and cut them off in the
rear. The order was promptly obeyed, three boat's crews to the best of my
knowledge composing the latter force, namely Spartan's Launches and Barac-
outa and Macedonian's Pinnaces, the command devolving upon the First
Lieutenant of the Spartan. Although we used all possible speed in making the
ascent we were too late to accomplish fully our object, a small valley in the rear
of the fort, which terminated in a ravine, having facilitated them in making
good their retreat beyond the reach of capture, but still within good musket
range, and we immediately commenced firing again upon them, giving chase
at the same time. In the course of an hour or more our forces became so scattered over the hills, as to cause danger to each other from our own fire;
seeing this the officers recalled their men and descending the hills again
formed our men in the valley below, and putting them in motion proceeded up
the same, when I met the Am. Consul who called my attention to two or three
guns, two and four pounders and one gingall, which he claimed as having
secured in the fort, after it was taken. It was whilst attempting to drag these
pieces down to the landing, that John Morrison, seaman, received a wound
in the head from what I think was a gingall ball, from the size and appearance
of the wound, he died before he could be conveyed to the ship. From this time
until our return on board our operations were confined to the destruction of such
property as might hereafter be of any service to the Pirates, and to the conveyance of such guns from the shore to the boat, as could be carried by the
men.*

*In concluding my report it is but just to say that the division of men under
my command composed of the crew of the Macedonian's Pinnace behaved in an
orderly, steady manner deserving of all praise. As to the number of Pirates
killed during the action, it is difficult to say, from my own observation and
that of other officers, I should think the number exceeded thirty-five and was
less than fifty.*

Very respectfully, Your Obt. Servant

LIEUTENANT COMMANDING,   *(signed)* J. GLENDY SPROSTON

GEO. HENRY PREBLE, U.S.N.,   *Acting Master, U.S.N.*

U.S. STEAMER *Queen.*

§4. OFFICIAL RECORDS OF THE UNION AND CONFEDERATE NAVIES IN THE WAR OF THE REBELLION

Series 1, v. 4:

April 27, 1861. Lieutenant John Glendy Sproston, Commanding U.S.S. *Powhatan* in the Washington Navy Yard.

April 28. He was ordered to proceed down the Potomac to replace and protect the buoys at the Kettle Bottom Shoals, which have been removed.

May 1. After performing his duty, he was back at the Washington Navy Yard.

May 4. He was ordered to proceed to Fort Monroe with the dispatches and return to Washington again. He returned on May 9th.

May 14. Off Aqua Creek.

Series 1, v. 12:

February 19, 1862. Sproston was on the U.S.S. *Seneca* as the first lieutenant in Wright's River.

April 2. U.S.S. *Seneca* off Jacksonville, Florida.

May 3. At Mayport Mills, St. John's River, Florida.

June 8. Sproston killed.

U.S. GUNBOAT *Seneca*.

MAYPORT MILLS, ST. JOHN'S RIVER, FLA.

JUNE 8, 1862

Sir:

I have the melancholy duty to report the death of Lieutenant John G. Sproston, the executive officer of this vessel.

At 3.30 a.m. of to-day he left in command of three boats with Acting Master J. H. Rogers, Master's Mate Fiske, and 40 small armsmen. He was accompanied by a reserve force of 30 men from the Patroon.

The object was to capture a man named George Huston, a captain of a company of rebels now in the vicinity of Black Creek. I was informed that Huston boasted of having hung a negro pilot who was captured at the time of the death of Lieutenant Commanding Budd near Smyrna, and on that account I wished him as a prisoner, for the purpose of securing the general tranquility of persons along this river, most of whom, I doubt not, would gladly acknowledge the authority of the Government of the United States were they not in fear of violence from men of this character.

Lieutenant Sproston landed at early daylight and proceeded rapidly with his party to the house of Huston. The latter, it appears, was apprised of his coming and met him at the door armed with a double-barreled gun, two pistols, and bowie knife.

Upon the demand of Lieutenant Sproston to surrender himself as prisoner, Huston fired at him with a pistol, the ball entering high up on the left breast and killing him instantly. Huston discharged the other pistol and gun without further injury to our party and was instantly wounded in four places and brought on board. He is supposed to be mortally wounded. Several shots were fired from Huston's house by persons who escaped.

It is needless for me to state to you and to the Department the character of Lieutenant Sproston, known as he is as a highly accomplished and honorable officer. I can not refrain, however, from expressing my deep regret that the country should have lost so valuable an officer by the hand of a miscreant.

> (*signed*) DANIEL AMMEN
> *Lieut. Comdg. and Senior Officer of Forces*
> *in St. John's River.*
> *Flag-officer Samuel F. Du Pont*
> *Comdg. South Atlantic Blockading Squadron,*
> *Port Royal, S. C."*

June 27. George Huston, the murderer of Lieutenant Sproston, died from the effects of his wounds on the 19th instant.

June......'An able, brave and devoted officer from the state of Maryland.' From a letter of Rear-Admiral S. F. Du Pont.

April 28, 1863. '......Lieutenant Sproston, one of my best and earliest friends, and with whom I was for eight years a messmate.' From a letter of Lieutenant-Commander Kidder Randolph Breese to Rear-Admiral D. D. Porter.

§5. OFFICE MEMORANDA

'*John Glendy Sproston, distinguished while in command of one of the boats which destroyed the rebel privateer under the guns of Pensacola Navy Yard in September 1861 and his whole conduct during this war has been gallant and meritorious*'. Office of Naval Records and Library, Navy Department.

§6. MARYLAND GENERAL ASSEMBLY
Resolution no. 8 Act of 1862

Sproston, John Glendig [sic]—1862.
  Midshipman, 15 July, 1846; Passed Midshipman, 8 June, 1852;
  Master, 15 September, 1855; Lieutenant, 16 September, 1855; killed,
  8 June, 1862.

Resolved, That the thanks of the Legislature of Maryland are due, and hereby tendered to Lieutenant John H. Russell, a native of Montgomery county, in this State, for his gallantry and daring in running into Pensacola harbor, directly under the guns of the enemy, and firing and destroying the Rebel Pirate Judith; *and that in connection with the name of Lieutenant Russell, that of Lieutenant John Glendig Sproston, of the City of Baltimore, be associated......*

*Original Manuscript Journal of the Opening of Japan by an Officer of Perry's
Squadron.*

*550. SPROSTON (JOHN GLENDY). Original manuscript journal kept
during Perry's expedition to Japan, beginning February 1854 at Yeddo
Bay and ending August 1854 at Manila Bay. 105 pp., folio, original half
calf.*

*A highly important personal narrative of the signing of the Treaty which
opened the ports of Japan to the outside world, made by a passed Midshipman of the* Macedonian, *one of Perry's famous fleet.*

*Interspersed throughout the journal are eighteen original pencil and pen-and-
ink sketches of Japanese scenes, boats, wrestling matches, etc., including one
of a reception given by Captains Adams and Abbott to the Japanese authorities on board ship, and in which the author took part.*

*Several pages tell of the Macedonians' voyage among the islands of Japan
when separated from the fleet, and contain much information not recorded in
Perry's* Narrative.

*After leaving Japan the ship visited Formosa and Lieut. Breeze [sic] of the
same ship, has inserted a three page description of his visit to the coal mines
of that island. Sproston also gives a long and interesting account of the
fleet at Manila and of his adventures ashore.*

BIBLIOGRAPHY

American Sources

BARROWS, Edward Morley. *The Great Commodore; the Exploits of Matthew Calbraith Perry*. Indianapolis, 1935.

CUTLER, Carl C. *Greyhounds of the Sea; the American Clipper Ship*. New York, 1930.

..DAVIS, George Lynn-Lachlan. *A Paper upon the Origin of the Japan Expedition*. Read the 7th of May, 1857, before the Maryland Historical Society. (Annual Report of the President, 1860). Baltimore, 1860.

DENNET, Tyler. *Americans in Eastern Asia; a Critical Study of the Policy of the United States with Reference to China, Japan and Korea in the 19th Century*. New York, 1922.

GRIFFIS, William Elliot. *Matthew Calbraith Perry, a Typical American Naval Officer*. Boston, 1890.

———. *The Mikado's Empire*. New York, 1889.

HARRIS, Townsend. *The Complete Journal of Townsend Harris, First American Consul-General and Minister to Japan; Introduction and Notes* by Mario Emilio Cosenza. Garden City, N. Y., 1930.

LUBBOCK, Basil. *The China Clippers*. Glasgow, 1914.

PERRY, Matthew Calbraith. *Narrative of the Expedition of an American Squadron to the China Seas and Japan, Performed in the years 1852, 1853 and 1854, under the Command of Commodore M. C. Perry, United States Navy, by Order of the Government of the United States.* Washington, 1856. 3 v.

STARBUCK, Alexander. *History of the American Whale Fishery from its Earliest Inception to the Year 1876*. Waltham, Mass., 1878.

U.S. NAVY. *Official Records of the Union and Confederate Navies in the War of Rebellion*......Ser. I, v. 1-27; Ser. II, v, 1-3. Washington 1894–1922.

WILLIAMS, Frederick Wells. *The Life and Letters of Samuel Wells Williams, Missionary, Diplomat, Sinologue*. New York, 1889.

WILLIAMS, Samuel Wells. 'A Journal of the Perry Expedition to Japan.' *Transactions of the Asiatic Society of Japan*. v. 37, part 2, 1910.

Japanese Sources

Dai Nihon Komon Sho: Bakumatsu Gaikō Bunsho [Sources of Japanese History: Documents relating to Foreign Relations in the Last Days of the Tokugawa Shogunate. 1853–1854] v. 1-7. Tokyo, Tokyo Imperial University, 1910–1915.

——*Furoku* [Supplementary Volumes] 3 v. Tokyo, 1913–1921.

FOR FURTHER READING

BEASLEY, W. G. *Great Britain and the Opening of Japan. 1834–1858.* London: Luzac, 1951.

COLE, Allen B. (ed.) *A Scientist with Perry in Japan: the Journal of Dr. James Morrow.* Chapel Hill: University of North Carolina Press, 1947.

GRAFF, Henry F. (ed.) *Bluejackets with Perry in Japan; a day-by-day account kept by Master's Mate John R. C. Lewis and Cabin Boy William B. Allen.* New York: New York Public Library, 1952.

Heine, Wilhelm. *Reise um die Erde nach Japan an Bord der Expeditions-Escadre unter Commodore M.C. Perry in den Jahren 1853, 1854, und 1855, unternommen im Auftrage der Regierung der Vereinigten Staaten.* Leipzig: Dott Burfürft, 1856. 2 vols.

LENSEN, George Alexander. *Russia's Japan Expedition of 1852 to 1855.* Gainesville: University of Florida Press, 1955.

MORISON, Samuel E. *Old Bruin: Commodore Matthew C. Perry, 1794–1858.* Boston: Atlantic Monthly Press, 1967.

Statler, Oliver. *The Black Ship Scroll. An account of the Perry Expedition at Shimoda in 1854 and the lively beginnings of people-to-people relations between Japan and America.* Rutland, Vt.: Charles E. Tuttle Co., 1963.

SZCZESNIAK, Boleslaw (ed.) *The Opening of Japan. A Diary of Discovery in the Far East, 1853–1856.* By Rear Admiral George Henry Preble, U.S.N. Norman: University of Oklahoma Press, 1962.

WALLACH, Sidney (ed.) *Narrative of the Expedition of an American Squadron to the China Seas and Japan under the Command of Commodore M. C. Perry.* New York: Coward-McCann, 1952. (An abridgment of the original 3 vol. narrative.)

WALWORTH, Arthur Clarence. *Black Ships off Japan; the story of Commodore Perry's Expedition.* New York: Alfred A. Knopf, 1946.

Index

DATE DU